COERCION

By
Paul Grant

By the same author

BERLIN: Caught in the Mousetrap – The Schultz Family Series 1

BERLIN: Reaping the Whirlwind – The Schultz Family Series 2

BERLIN: Uprising – The Schultz Family Series 3

COERCION

By
Paul Grant

© Paul Grant 2018

Paul Grant has asserted his rights under the Copyright, Designs and Patents Act, 1988, to be identified as the author of this work.

This novel is a work of fiction and, except in the case of historical fact, any resemblance to actual persons, living or dead, is purely coincidental.

Thanks, as always to Hayley.
For Millie.

PROLOGUE

LATE AUGUST 1961, EAST BERLIN

The late summer sun blazed through the hospital window, forcing Hans Erdmann to shield his eyes. The sheets were starch-stiff, and the air had a whiff of disinfectant. He reached for a glass of water to rid his mouth of the metallic taste. He had no reason to complain about his treatment because it had been first class. The doctors and nurses had taken care of him as if it were Ulbricht himself lying there. Then again, the story the authorities had managed to concoct, and continued to peddle, had been something of a fairy tale.

The nurse said something, dragging Hans back to reality.

'Sorry?'

'I'll let your visitor know you're awake, Comrade Colonel.'

'Visitor?'

She'd already left. Hans thought he could smell tobacco smoke.

The door to his room was ajar. A languid man slid through the gap, taking the last puffs on his cigarette.

'Thank you, sir.' It was the nurse's voice, patience wearing thin.

'My apologies, Nurse.' The man smiled briefly, grinding out the cigarette in the proffered ash tray. 'You're still with us then, Erdmann?'

Hans turned towards the window and sighed. 'What do you want, Burzin?'

Burzin closed the door; nobody could hear this conversation. He said in hushed tones, 'That's a nice welcome for a man who helped you in your hour of need.'

'Not that it did me much good.'

Hans couldn't help feeling alone and as bad as he'd felt since leaving Leipzig behind all those years ago. He'd been running away from the pain and tragedy, then; now it was something else.

Burzin walked around the bed towards the window. 'Perhaps not, but I thought you'd like to know your comrade is in the West and recovering well.'

'Bernie's okay?' Hans said.

'The last I heard.'

Hans sighed, relief coursing through him. It had been worth it after all.

'It doesn't look like you have too much to complain about, though. This must be the best room the Charité has to offer.' Burzin was fiddling with the handle of the window, one eye on the door.

'Nothing to complain about, except I'm still in East Berlin.'

'Things could have been a hell of a lot worse for you, Erdmann. Not only are you still alive, your enemies are off your back, for now at least, and everybody thinks you're a hero. What's your problem?'

Hans shook his head. He knew he'd been fortunate. He could easily be dead, or in Bautzen or Hohenschönhausen, though it didn't make him feel any brighter.

Burzin had managed to open the window. He'd lit a cigarette and was trying unsuccessfully to exhale through the narrow aperture. He turned briefly. 'You have to think about the future now.'

Hans looked towards the door, then hissed, 'The future? I don't have a future here.'

Burzin tutted. 'You don't think they're going to let one of their heroes go so easily, do you? They'll be watching you, Hans. You didn't get out of this one totally unblemished.'

The prick of concern he felt told Hans his body was starting to recover.

'You're just going to have to bide your time and trust me.'

Hans scoffed.

Burzin flicked his half-finished cigarette out of the window and moved towards the bed, his face serious now. 'You're forgetting who delivered your friend to you and gave you the opportunity to escape…'

'…Sorting out one of your own problems at the same time.'

'The Schultz girl?' Burzin shrugged. 'One good turn deserves another.'

'Exactly, and now we're even.'

Burzin shook his head. 'It doesn't work like that and you know it.'

There was silence between them. Hans could hear the bustle of a busy hospital out on the corridor: snapped instructions, a shout for assistance, and from nowhere a cackling laugh which disintegrated into a long, chesty hack.

Burzin was over his momentary outburst and was now offering heartfelt advice. 'Be patient. Stay calm and do nothing that will alert them.' He smiled, but there was little warmth. 'We'll work something out.'

Hans disliked the man intensely, but he knew Burzin was right.

CHAPTER 1

MAY 1962, WEST BERLIN

As Gerd Braun gunned his scooter and headed back towards Kreuzberg, his mind was firmly fixed on his dilemma. He smiled as he weaved through the traffic. It had only been flirting at first. He did his best to get the exact magazines she asked for. She was a customer after all, yet he found himself going that extra distance to please her. He couldn't help himself, which wasn't really like him. Things had progressed, and even when they put a barrier in their way, he found a way around it. His feelings for her had grown strong, so much so he was scared that he couldn't control them. That's what had led him into the shady world of the escape organisations.

His scooter parked, Gerd made his way on foot towards Heidelberger Strasse. He reached the street where some children were swarming around a football as if passing to each other were out of the question. An old lady, an apron spread across her ample front, cast a watchful eye over them from a doorway, offering sharp words of maternal guidance when the game became too rough for her liking. It was any normal street scene, all, that is, except for the wall – more than two metres high, topped off with a "Y" frame of barbed wire for good measure. Such was the haste with which the breeze blocks had been placed, there were small crevices through which the guards could be seen constantly patrolling on the other side. Further down the street, where the apartments ended on the junction of Treptower Strasse, stood a wooden watchtower.

The street the kids were playing on was actually East German territory; the doorframe against which the old lady leant was the real border. To the uninitiated it was a crazy situation, but to Gerd, and the kids, this was everyday life. It had been so for nine months now. The wall which divided Heidelberger Strasse was here to stay; the East Germans, backed by the Russians, were not going to relent.

Gerd doubled back away from the border, avoiding the prying eyes of the Vopos and the Stasi. Finally, he entered the Krug pub from Elsenstrasse. It was only late afternoon, but the place was still rowdy. He winced at the din. The early shift at the police station had kicked out. A group of West Berlin policemen were in animated conversation, their pointed helmets on the table amongst numerous glasses, most of them spent. He didn't usually feel comfortable so close to the law of the land, but in this instance, he accepted it; the real enemy was just on the other side of the block wall, not ten metres from the door of the pub.

Lemmer, the landlord, caught his eye and flicked his head towards the back. Gerd went to the end of the bar and lifted the counter. As he slipped into the back room, nobody batted an eyelid, so used were the locals to the comings and goings.

In the back, Walther Noltke was in full flow, haranguing the Stasi "filth", the others watching on. Gerd smiled to himself as he took up a place at the table against the wall, an overflowing ashtray rested precariously on a stack of old accounting books by his elbow.

Walther nodded a brief acknowledgment towards Gerd. 'And so, I come to the point of dragging you reprobates here.'

There was nervous laughter. Jürgen, thin and scrawny, was star struck, his eyes glazed, reflecting like a pair of mirrors. Peter, more of a thinker, listened intently. The thick-set Arno filled the threadbare armchair, nervously puffing cigarette smoke into the air.

'Next weekend is the holiday,' Walther started. 'We need to be through by then.'

Confusion reigned. It was typical of Noltke, his mind working overtime. They didn't know him like Gerd. If you didn't join the dots, you got left behind.

Arno sighed. 'Through where?'

Walther tutted dramatically. 'To the other side.'

So, they were going to be tunnelling again.

'Where do we start from?' Gerd asked, trying to move things along.

Walther smiled, seemingly happy somebody was keeping up. He took a swig from his apple juice. 'Right here,' he said.

'From the pub?' Peter asked, open-mouthed.

'Well, the cellar.'

Arno raised an eyebrow. 'Coming out where?'

'The photography shop on the corner.'

Jürgen whistled. 'Right under their noses.'

Walther shrugged nonchalantly. 'The best way.'

Walther Noltke had gained his fame as a champion East German swimmer, but more recently as a daring *Fluchthelfer*. It wasn't the first time they'd used Heidelberger Strasse. The apartment blocks were so close that the inhabitants would talk to each other from their respective balconies.

Arno looked doubtful. It was the first tunnel since it had happened. 'And do the shop owners know? Are they in?'

Walther tutted again.

Gerd had it worked out. 'The holiday weekend.'

Walther slapped his thigh excitedly. 'Exactly! From Friday afternoon to Tuesday morning the place will be empty. Imagine how many we could get out in that time.'

He pulled a piece of paper from his pocket. 'I started to make a list. Peter, your wife and son, your sister. Arno, your brother and mother. Jürgen, your parents and your brother.' Walther turned to Gerd. 'Your girl as well.'

Gerd felt his stomach leap with excitement. It was real now they had a target date.

'We need more names. I want fifty,' Walther said.

'Fifty? Are you mad?' It was Arno. 'We'll never get away with it. The Vopos are up and down past that shop window every five minutes.'

'Then we'll have to make it work.' Walther's eyes were fierce now. They all knew why. 'We will make it work. As many as possible.'

The room was filled by a sober silence. They'd all noticed the crack in his voice. Arno was staring at Gerd, his eyes a little bit wider, more intense than before.

Gerd shrugged. There was no point in saying anything, not now anyway. Even if he left it until later, until Walther had calmed down, there would be no point. He wouldn't relent.

'Now, the equipment from the last dig is already downstairs. I have organised some mattresses, so we can sleep down there. We stay in there and don't come out until we're through. All agreed?'

There was concurrence in the room. The need for security was stronger than ever, especially after what happened to Hans.

'Okay. I suggest you all use the weekend to take some rest and to get messages to your loved ones; no details for their own good, only when they need to be ready.'

Walther was quiet now, his apparent excitement at sharing his plan done.

Peter got up and Jürgen followed suit. Arno stayed where he was in the armchair, seemingly uncertain. 'Are you sure it's not too soon?' he ventured cautiously.

The others stopped, watching Walther for his response. He was facing the fireplace, head bowed, hands on the mantelpiece, his back to them.

Gerd feared an explosion of anger. He'd been prone to that since it happened.

This time his words were barely audible. 'I don't know, Arno. I really don't know.' Then he turned, full of energy once again. 'But people are relying on us to come through. So, we do it.'

His conviction was strong, his focus seemingly total.

Arno nodded, but still appeared unsure.

'Take care on the way out. Leave in stages, not all together. Remember, they're always watching this place.'

Gerd sighed; the excitement had given way to a wave of dread. He had the weekend to convince her. It might be his last chance.

CHAPTER 2

MAY 1962, EAST BERLIN

Above everything else, Miriam Hirsch admired her mother's strength of character. Nothing seemed to faze her. She was one of the few people who the party types actually seemed scared of. Hannah Hirsch was one of the original members of the Committee for the Victims of Fascism, having been one herself. She'd joined the Communist Party in late 1945 and had been active in the party since then. Even though she was only in her late thirties, Hannah Hirsch was almost an institution in East Berlin.

Her mother bustled into the room, searching for something, her shoes clipping urgently on the wooden floorboards.

'Now I have to go for a lecture. Please make sure you finish your homework and don't forget it's FDJ night tonight.'

Miriam groaned. 'I've told you, I don't want to go there any more.'

'Nonsense. Comradeship is good for the spirit. You always enjoy it when you make the effort to go.'

Miriam shook her head. There was no point in arguing with her mother's tried and tested witticisms.

'Miriam, I am talking to you.'

'You're not, you're talking *at* me.'

Her mother paused, then walked over to her by the window. 'Are you okay, dear? You seem miles away.'

'I'm fine. I'm just bored of these stupid youth meetings.'

'It'll be summer soon and then you'll be off camping. You always enjoy that.'

Miriam nodded resignedly. She turned back, catching her mother's eye, watching over her. It was times like this Miriam felt she could see straight through her.

'You've not seen that boy, have you?'

Miriam turned away in a huff. She hated being questioned.

Her mother bent at her knees, taking hold of her hand. 'It's important, Miriam, for your future. You understand what I'm saying to you?'

Miriam knew how it went. "Stay away from the 'rowdies' and 'antisocial elements' if you want to get on." Her mother didn't actually say it for once.

'No, Mother, not recently.'

'Good.' She tapped her knee. 'Best to keep it like that.' She stood to her full height and put her hand under Miriam's chin. 'I'll be back late tonight. See you later.' She kissed her tenderly on the forehead.

With that, her mother swept from the room, grabbing her satchel as she went.

Miriam sighed as she looked down on the Pankow street. People stood waiting patiently for the tram. Her life was so straightforward, like everything had been mapped out for her. She was in her final year at school and then university beckoned, destined to follow in her mother's footsteps; Hannah Hirsch, the senior professor at Humboldt University. It was all so dull and predictable. Her mother had warned, in the way only her mother could, that the grass wasn't always greener on the other side; she meant on the other side of the anti-fascist protection barrier, but didn't say that.

Before the city was divided, Miriam had loved her trips into the western sectors of Berlin. It didn't matter to her if it was the British or American sector; there was more life, more action. She visited her relatives in Dahlem and they would play in the Grunewald. Life was so much brighter compared to here, no matter what her mother said, or indeed, how convincingly she said it.

The beige tram had arrived; people got off, people got on. Monotonous life continued. She wanted something else. Ever since she'd met the cheeky Gerd Braun she was smitten. She missed him. His life was everything hers wasn't, or wasn't able to be. He was never short of an answer, able to get things done with a smile on his face. She had known he would leave for the West, and it was just like him to get the timing exactly right. It was early August last year when he had left, just a week before Ulbricht closed the hatch.

Of course, to her mother he was a risk, something to knock her off course. To Miriam he was a chance for a different life away from the dreary streets of the eastern sector. Maybe her mother was right. Maybe West Berlin and the capitalist world was a dangerous place, but Miriam couldn't help yearning for some of that uncertainty, some of that excitement.

Gerd had been to see her many times since the wall had gone up. When they stopped the West Berliners coming over, he had a West German passport within days. He was still only sixteen, but he always seemed to have the means. Then he dropped the bombshell: if it was what she really wanted, he could arrange it.

Her mother knew something was wrong, of course. Miriam's head had been in the clouds and Hannah Hirsch didn't miss a trick. Miriam wasn't sure yet if she could, or even wanted to go.

It would be risking a lot, everything, but the excitement of that thought wouldn't go away.

She had lied to her mother.

She would meet Gerd Braun tonight; the FDJ could keep.

CHAPTER 3

APRIL 1962, EAST BERLIN

The tram came to a juddering stop at Strausberg Nord station. Hans Erdmann joined the others alighting, mainly young men sporting unwieldy packs, chattering in anticipation of their first days of training. He had recovered physically. On cold days like this, he sometimes felt discomfort around the wound, but he was fit to return to duty. Summoned, as he had been, to NVA headquarters, he was soon to find out what his new duties would be.

'Colonel Erdmann!' A young officer looked past the fresh intake towards him.

'Follow me, please, Comrade Colonel.'

He was led to a *Kübelwagen* and driven away at speed. Hans slipped his hands into his greatcoat as the wind whipped his face. They passed a troop of tiring men, a bawling instructor seemingly fresh as a daisy beside them. He wondered what job they could give him. It would have nothing to do with the border; those days were done now, not that Hans was disappointed by that.

Most of the site had been expanded by the Nazis in the 1930s, and now it was being added to again. The main headquarters building, however, was older, Prussian in appearance. Hans was soon seated in a foyer area with a high ceiling, the emblem of the NVA tiled into the floor. His driver had gone off to inform Generalmajor Riedel of Hans's arrival. Whatever was coming, Hans didn't feel any excitement. His heart wasn't in it; that much hadn't changed since his enforced period of convalescence. 'Comrade Colonel, this way, please.'

They passed through a small anteroom and on into a larger room. A man was seated at the desk, younger than Hans; photographs with dignitaries littered the wall behind him. The man didn't stand. He merely looked up.

'I'm Generalmajor Riedel. Take a seat.'

The formal, stiff tone took him by surprise; he was used to more warmth from his commanding officers. The man in front of him was immaculate, his uniform pristine, his hair perfectly styled. Was Hans looking at the future of the Volksarmee?

'Thank you for coming here today, Erdmann. I know things have been difficult for you, but rest assured, the DDR appreciates your sacrifices.'

Things hadn't changed much. He was still being treated as a hero, as if the real events of that wet August evening of the previous year had been rewritten.

'Now you are fit for duty, I wanted to inform you of your new posting.' Riedel's eyes didn't flicker. There was no charm, no inflection. He might have been reading from a script.

'As you know, conscription is coming to the Democratic Republic. All eighteen- to twenty-six-year-olds will have to serve in the NVA.'

Hans knew it wouldn't have been possible before the wall went up. Such an announcement would have led to a stampede for the border.

'How does that affect me, Generalmajor?'

Riedel took a deep breath and slowly swept a hand through his hair.

'You will take up a new post sifting the conscripts for officer material.'

Hans coughed, failing to hide his shock.

Riedel's eyes were wide, as if he were offended. 'This is a very important role, Erdmann. Setting the right example is vital for our young conscripts.' He waved his hand. 'There will be rough edges to smooth, and I'm sure you're the right man to do it.'

Hans thought about it for a moment. He wondered if Riedel knew just what kind of example Hans had set.

'So, do you accept?'

'Do I have a choice?'

'I believe our young conscripts will be inspired by a hero of the DDR. You should accept, Erdmann.'

He felt wary, but he knew there were worse jobs. His mind had to be occupied with something until Burzin came up with a plan.

'I accept, Generalmajor.'

'Excellent. The *leutnant* has all the details.'

Hans stood up to leave.

'One more thing before you go. I would like you to perform an additional task.'

'Generalmajor?'

'You are to report to Humboldt University. It seems some philosophy students would like to hear from one of the brave soldiers protecting our borders.' Riedel smiled. 'It would be an excellent opportunity to showcase what we do, Erdmann. Let's call it a personal favour.'

Hans felt a twinge of concern; instinct. He wondered if Riedel knew something, yet the man didn't seem capable of sarcasm.

'I'm sorry, Generalmajor,' Hans said, confused.

'You are to report to this senior professor. The details are all there.'

He handed Hans a piece of paper. Hans stared at it, perturbed, then looked up, slightly open-mouthed.

'You can go, Erdmann.'

CHAPTER 4

MAY 1962, WEST BERLIN

Café Kranzler was buzzing in the spring sunshine. The constant hum of chatter was interspersed with laughter and the chink of teaspoons on crockery. There was barely a seat to be had on the packed forecourt. A bus passed by, the open-decked top thronged with tourists hungry for a piece of the Ku'damm. A beige Volkswagen followed in the bus's wake, its spluttering engine backfiring twice.

Gerd felt the intense stare of his friend Jack Kaymer. 'So, *what* have you been up to?'

Gerd couldn't help smiling, recalling the time when the two of them had first met. It had always been somewhat of a game between them. 'You know me well enough not to ask questions like that.'

Jack was looking at him strangely. 'Well, you've been occupied, I know that.' Jack was swirling the remnants of his coffee.

'You'll always be one step behind me, Jack.'

Despite the façade, Gerd felt anxious. He wasn't really in the mood for their normal japes and perhaps Jack had sensed it.

'Is that why I had to go all the way to Spandau to get hold of you?'

Gerd shrugged. 'All right, I admit I've been busy.'

'I'm not prying,' Jack said.

'It wouldn't get you very far.'

'Maybe not, but I do know there's something rattling around that brain of yours.'

Gerd didn't want to explain what he was feeling. He didn't want to explain that he was worried what Miriam would say when he told her about the tunnel. He couldn't talk about it to Jack, or anybody outside their small group.

'I'm fine.'

'Really? Yet we've been sat here half an hour and you've not once asked me why I came all the way to your uncle's to find you. You've not asked me once what's in it for Gerd Braun.'

His reputation as a wheeler-dealer went before him. He'd helped the American find what he was looking for the previous summer. They'd broken into the warehouse in Lichtenberg and had found it full of concrete posts and barbed wire. It had helped Jack, as a journalist, piece together his story about the intentions of the East German regime. It had told Gerd it was time to get out of the eastern sector. Gerd made good money on that deal, yet both of them had received more than they bargained for in the end, especially Jack.

'I've got something on my mind,' Gerd said, averting his gaze.

Jack lifted his eyebrows quickly. 'You don't say?'

'What?'

Jack shrugged.

'It's not like that,' Gerd said defensively.

'I never said a word.'

'No, but I know what you're thinking.'

'So, in addition to your nefarious skills, you're a mind reader as well.'

Gerd had grown bored of the playful teasing. 'So, what do you want?'

Jack was looking at him intently again. 'I wanted to talk to you about tunnels.'

Gerd's eyes widened. Did Jack know something or was he just fishing? Gerd shot a look over his shoulder. 'Do you want to keep your voice down?'

'No need to be so jumpy.'

'Come on, Jack, you of all people know what it's like. There are *Spitzel* everywhere, especially in West Berlin.'

This was the reason the two of them had talked in the first place; the signs warning of loose tongues at the refugee centre at Marienfelde. Jack had been there researching an article for his magazine.

'So, why the question?'

'I happen to have a contact who's interested in talking to the *Fluchthelfer*.'

'Are you sure it's not you?' Gerd said sarcastically. He could hear Walther's warning ringing in his ears. Jack was a good friend, and Gerd trusted him, but the fewer people that knew about Heidelberger Strasse, the better.

'I have to admit it would be a good story, but it's not really my thing.'

'That doesn't sound like the Jack Kaymer I know.'

'I need to help somebody. So, if you know someone…'

'Well, I don't,' Gerd snapped. He instantly felt guilty now he'd said it. He knew it made him look shifty, yet he was struggling to understand why Jack was asking these questions, especially now.

Jack raised an eyebrow, fiddling with a sachet of sugar as he did. Gerd turned his head towards the road. Close by, a woman yelped as her companion spilt coffee over the table.

'Do you want to talk about it?' Jack asked finally.

Gerd thought about it. He did, more than anything, but he couldn't. There was time for that after the event.

An awkward silence hung between the two of them, before Jack finally stood.

'You know where I am if you need me.'

Again, Gerd wanted to say something, but knew he couldn't. He only shook his head.

Jack threw some coins on the table, leaving Gerd to face his fears alone.

CHAPTER 5

MAY 1962, EAST BERLIN

Hans suspected it was a warning. No matter how the pompous Riedel has dressed it up as his idea, he knew it wasn't the case. This came from above. They were watching, and for now, he just had to play along.

He strode through the gates of Humboldt University's main building on the Unter den Linden. He'd chosen not to wear his uniform, not wanting to give whoever had organised this charade further satisfaction. The blue banner of the FDJ was draped from the front of the building, next to it a large portrait of Ulbricht on a red background, just in case anybody was in doubt who was running the place. The architecture inside was impressive. Hans couldn't help smiling; even Ulbricht would struggle to deny the Prussian influence in the decor.

He was pointed towards a central staircase, all marble and granite. The office he was looking for was on the second floor, according to the helpful attendant. As Hans checked along the large dark doors for the correct office, he had to wonder what he was doing there.

He found the name he'd been given embossed on a brass plate with severe-looking typography. Reluctantly, he knocked on the door.

'Enter!' It was a woman's voice.

Hans pushed on the door. It opened but was stopped half way by an obstruction. He slid through the gap to see a box overflowing with books, preventing the door moving any further.

There were books and files stacked in every conceivable place. Shelves were crammed to bursting point.

'Don't mind the mess. Come in, come in,' the woman said. She was perched on the edge of her desk in the only space available. She looked to be in her late thirties, dark hair, and – Hans noticed, somewhat surprised – attractive.

He would have expected someone older to blend in with the surroundings; dust particles swirled in a shaft of sunlight over her shoulder. Hans felt slightly uncomfortable. He was used to order, everything in its place.

The woman was looking at him expectantly, bright eyes wide.

'Er… Hans Erdmann,' he said, offering his hand.

The woman touched her head. 'Ah yes, I completely forgot.' It didn't put her off her stride. She took his hand in a firm grip, looking him directly in the eye. 'Hannah Hirsch.'

He looked around, wondering where he might sit himself amongst the chaos, but seemingly that wasn't the plan.

'I usually take my morning constitutional around this time. Would you care to join me?'

The direct approach almost caught him off guard, then he shrugged. 'Maybe it's better; there might be more space outside.'

She laughed. 'A room without books is like a body without a soul, Herr Erdmann.'

Grabbing her jacket, she motioned towards the door. 'Do you read?'

They were on the corridor now, every sound echoing. He wondered if this was part of an interrogation and that the only answer should be, "Neues Deutschland", but decided to deflect the question. 'My job doesn't allow much time.'

'Yet you had time recently… with your injuries.'

Wary, he glanced at her as they walked side by side.

Seemingly she sensed it. 'Forgive my directness, Herr Erdmann. My daughter tells me it unnerves her.'

He nodded, with a half-smile, believing her daughter to be a good judge.

'I read it in the newspapers when I was asked to meet you,' she explained.

They reached the stairway. He wondered exactly who had made the request, but a busy stairway wasn't the time or the place. He chose to revert to the original question.

'I've never been one for books, Frau Hirsch…'

'Call me Hannah. I'm not one for formality.'

'My life has been taken up by the military, Hannah.'

'No family?'

He paused before shaking his head. Even the candid Hannah Hirsch seemed to realise it wasn't a subject to touch. 'Shall we walk on the Lustgarten?'

'Fine with me.' He felt better away from the academic stuffiness of the university. Out on the main boulevard, the sun was shining. They walked by the old baroque building of the Zeughaus towards the cathedral.

'My rector felt it would be useful for you to meet my students. Last year we discussed the need for the barrier. He felt one of the men who led the border brigades would be able to help them understand the policy. I am grateful you agreed.'

Hans raised his eyebrows.

'You didn't agree?'

'Not exactly.' Hans looked to his left, noticing the reconstruction work on the Altes Museum.

'I sense reluctance,' Hannah said, looking at him intently. He pursed his lips, wondering if she actually knew why.

'I'm not sure I'm cut out to address a group of students. It's not really my thing.'

She smiled. 'What? A colonel in our great Volksarmee is scared of talking to a few students?'

He laughed, accepting her teasing in good spirits.

They strolled on past people enjoying the sunshine. Hans breathed more freely. 'You've worked at the university a long time?'

'Since just after the war,' she said.

'And during the war?'

She stopped and looked at him. 'I am Jewish, Hans.'

He should have realised. He closed his eyes for a moment, feeling stupid. 'I'm sorry. I…'

She shook it off very easily. 'I had a better war than most,' she said. 'It gives one a sense of focus and perspective.'

Even if she may have been part of all this, Hans couldn't help admiring the woman. The scarred buildings and wide-open spaces caused by the war were all around them. They only hinted at the human cost. Hannah had apparently dealt with it and come out of the other side. Hans was not sure he could say the same for himself.

She tilted her head whilst she looked at him. 'So, will the Volksarmee colonel meet my students?'

He felt something inside him. Emotions stirred. He was shocked by it. This woman was interesting. She was also dangerous, yet he couldn't help the half-smile that formed on his lips.

'I'll think about it.'

CHAPTER 6

MAY 1962, WEST BERLIN

Gerd Braun approached the checkpoint on Heinrich Heine Strasse. Guards hovered by the small opening for pedestrians to the right. He felt for the passport in his pocket; it was his lifeline to East Berlin, his only way to Miriam. His eyes were drawn to the floor as he reached the whitewashed, stacked railway sleepers. The tramlines in the centre of the road were abruptly cut by the wall. This was the border.

Away to his left, a young couple stood on the elevated platform, peering over into East Berlin. He found it strange that if somebody placed a barrier of some kind in the way, human nature forced one to want to peer over it, or even pass through it.

Gerd handed over the West German passport to the armed guard. This was the designated crossing point for West Germans. West Berliners were not permitted to go to East Berlin without a visa, which were only given in rare circumstances, if at all.

The young guard gave it cursory glance then waved him through; he knew the real inspection would come some metres further on. As Gerd passed through the opening, there was a wall to his right and a road to his left. A car passed him, slaloming between the blocks; they'd only been recently placed there. A man had tried to ram through the checkpoint using a truck laden with sand. He got through, but died later after being shot a number of times then buried by the load behind him. Gerd grimaced at the thought.

He always came here on foot. Not wanting to arouse suspicion, he thought the scooter was too recognisable. A uniformed officer now thumbed his passport. His movements were deliberately slow, fostering nervousness and fear. The passport was in a false name, but it was professionally made. Gerd knew it, because it had passed the test many times before.

The passport was stamped and slid under the glass; a visa had been added to be returned on exit. Gerd nodded at the officer, a guard opened the gate and he slipped into East Berlin. The tramlines magically reappeared from under the barrier. Just further on, a tram disgorged its passengers at the terminus. People bustled towards the barrier heading west. Gerd turned and looked around him, wary of a tail, before heading east.

He consciously started at a leisurely pace over the Spree and the railway lines, meandering in the rough direction of Alexanderplatz. He stopped to look up the river, east towards Treptow. He noticed nothing out of the ordinary. There were no sudden changes of direction, nobody stopping to admire the view as he had done. There could have been more than one of them, of course.

Closer to Alexanderplatz, Gerd nipped off the main street towards Strausberger Platz and Karl-Marx-Allee. He had time before he met her and wanted to be entirely certain he wasn't being followed. He pulled up the collar of his jacket, feeling a chill as it headed towards evening, or perhaps it was just the thought of being in East Berlin again. Again, he slowed, then crossed the road and headed back in the opposite direction. By now, he was confident there was no tail.

Strausberger Platz and the start of Karl-Marx-Allee was now on his right. The building site in front of him had caused an argument with Miriam during his last visit. She'd proudly told him it was to be the site of a large cinema complex. He'd snapped at her, 'There are cinemas in West Berlin, you know?'

Her face had registered the shock and he'd regretted it immediately. The pressure of the whole thing was getting to him.

Gerd finally reached Alexanderplatz. Cars waited at lights on the roundabout as trams criss-crossed the centre of the gigantic square. The Berolina Haus on the right, the HO department store to the left, and poking between the two, the Rotes Rathaus visible above the railway bridge, a large advertisement for the *Neues Deutschland* spanning it. Propaganda posters ringed the square reminding East Berliners this was their capital. Even if it wasn't his favourite place, at least the number of people around provided a cloak of anonymity.

Then he saw her and felt that rush inside him. He knew why he was there. Pretty with style, bright and sharp in an endearing way, Miriam Hirsch had grabbed his attention that first day. She saw him and her eyes lit up like they did, sucking him in like nobody else had. They hugged each other close for a moment, then they were facing each other. He gave her a light peck on the cheek and they giggled. It was still young love, smitten yet slightly awkward. Gerd glanced over his shoulder.

'Come on, let's walk.'

Nothing was said between them. All the anticipation had been building to this. It was always like that at first during their grabbed moments – illicit, yet at the same time incredibly innocent. Words would never be enough.

Finally, she said nervously, 'I am supposed to be at the FDJ meeting tonight.'

Gerd had to shake himself. He was operating in a different world, far from meetings feeding teenagers with propaganda, but he didn't show it. It wasn't her fault.

'I'm glad you didn't go.' He noticed his cheeks were aching due to the constant smiling.

'It's so dull. I hate it.'

'Try not to cause trouble with your mum; it won't be long now.'

She stopped and turned to him. 'When?'

He sighed, not sure he wanted to say. 'This weekend, all being well.'

He could see the colour drain from her face, just like it had when he'd first voiced the idea. It unnerved him, just like it had then. 'Are you okay? You look shocked.'

'It's just that…'

Miriam appeared confused and torn. It was why he was reluctant to tell her, but what choice did he have? He took her arm and they walked on.

'I find it really difficult to think about leaving Mother, and that's without considering the problems it would bring for her at work. You cannot imagine the shame of having a child who flees west.' She shook her head.

He wasn't big on family. He was an independent being, a lone operator. At least he thought he was, until he met Miriam.

'I know it's hard, but you have to think about the quality of life you will have over there. This place is dying around you.'

A train rumbled overhead, leaving the station, as they crossed the road. Miriam looked towards the ground, seemingly working things over in her mind.

'How will we get out?' she eventually said.

Gerd was wary of saying too much. 'A short tunnel.'

'Who is helping you, Gerd? Are these people reliable?'

'What do you mean "reliable"?'

'Well, it's just that these people have a very bad reputation here. Taking money in exchange for helping people, using guns.'

Gerd felt himself getting angry. 'These people are my friends, Miriam, and nobody is taking any money. They are people like you and me, just wanting to be reunited with loved ones they have been wrenched apart from. Do you think they'd put their families in any more danger than they have to?'

She seemed chastened by the strength of his response. 'I suppose not,' she said quietly.

He was feeling frustrated. He knew her mother had got inside her head. 'I wish you would just believe in me, Miriam.'

They passed the doors of the HO department store, already closed for the evening.

'It's not about belief, Gerd.' He could see the moisture forming in her eyes now. Her cheeks already glistened with the first tears. He pulled her close to his chest. Her cheeks were wet.

She sobbed, her body shaking. 'I just don't know if I can leave her.'

His heart sank, feeling her pain. Maybe it was his pain, too; Jack hadn't missed it in him. He didn't know what else to say, not without appearing to push her, and he didn't feel that was right. She had to make up her own mind. He also knew if she agreed now, she could well change her mind again later.

The time to convince her was running out, because from tomorrow night he would be digging non-stop until breakthrough.

Then it would be all systems go, and Miriam had to be ready to leave.

CHAPTER 7

MAY 1962, WEST BERLIN

As he made his way home through the evening traffic, Jack couldn't help thinking about Gerd. Their friendship had blossomed after an unlikely business deal, of which Jack wasn't exactly proud. That said, Gerd had taught him a thing or two about the art of negotiation. It was after that when the young man's true colours had risen to the surface. Jack hadn't forgotten what his friend had done for him, and he never would.

Mentioning escape tunnels at the café had been more than a game and Gerd's sensitivity had been illuminating. His journalist's nose sensed something. He was worried his friend was deep into something he couldn't control. Jack couldn't help thinking Gerd had wanted to tell him something earlier but couldn't.

He locked up the car and headed up to the apartment. For the first time that day he felt pangs of hunger. The sounds of a small child laughing brought him back to reality and instantly put a smile on his face. He pushed open the apartment door to see Tanja running towards him, squealing. Her top half seemed to be moving faster than her unsteady legs.

'Papa!' she shouted.

He managed to catch her before she fell on her face. He picked her up and spun her around which did little to stop the laughing.

'A sweet-smelling, squeaky clean daughter!' He held her up, all bathed and ready for bed. His wife, Eva, emerged from the bathroom, sporting a red face from the heat. Jack kissed her on the cheek. 'How's your day been?'

'Oh, you know, fun but tiring.' She tickled Tanja's foot. 'This little lady has a lot of energy.'

'It looks like it.' He smiled, squeezing Eva with his free arm.

'Dad called. He asked you to give him a ring when you got home.'

Jack laughed. 'It must be important if he's using the telephone.'

She hit him playfully on the chest. 'He's not that old-fashioned, Jack.'

He had the utmost respect for Eva's father, Klaus. He even liked him, but more often than not, he could be difficult to deal with.

'I'd better give him a call now.'

'I didn't get around to dinner yet,' Eva said.

'Don't worry, I'll head out and pick us something up later.'

He passed Tanja back and thought about fixing himself a drink but decided it could wait.

The phone seemed to be ringing for an age before it was answered. As usual the response was gruff.

'Schultz.'

'Klaus, it's Jack. How's it going?'

'Late.'

Jack laughed. 'I said to Eva it must be important if you were using the phone.'

'You thought right.'

'What's on your mind?'

'Did you think about what I said?' His voice had softened slightly.

'I did.' Jack sighed.

'And? Any progress?'

'Some. Look, Klaus, you know it's best not to say too much on the phone.'

Everyone knew all calls to West Berlin went through the East.

'That doesn't sound very promising.'

'I'm working on it, Klaus. I'll have something in a couple of weeks.'

'A couple of weeks? I thought you hacks were supposed to have all the contacts.'

Jack bristled at the slight to his professionalism. 'It's in hand, Klaus.'

There was silence at the other end of the line. Eva caught his eye, looking quizzically. Jack rolled his eyes, bringing a smile from her.

'I thought you might need a real Berliner to help you along.'

'Klaus, there's really no need…'

'I'm between jobs.' Klaus was a builder, working for himself. 'I've got a flight tomorrow. See you then.'

'Klaus…'

The line was dead.

Open-mouthed, Jack replaced the receiver.

CHAPTER 8

MAY 1962, EAST BERLIN

Miriam Hirsch made her way somewhat listlessly back to Pankow. She hoped her mother wasn't home, but just in case, she'd taken her time; she had to make it appear she'd been at the youth meeting.

Now she knew when she had to be ready to leave, it was all too real. She still hadn't made a decision to go or stay. Every time she convinced herself it was best for her future prospects to go west, she saw her mother's face. Miriam shuddered involuntarily; she knew the pain it would cause. She cared deeply for Gerd, maybe even loved him, but could she commit her future to him? These were two different decisions; one about fleeing East Germany, the other concerning Gerd Braun. She knew she could rely on her extended family in West Berlin if she did go, rather than pinning all her hopes and dreams on Gerd. She felt a twinge of guilt at how she'd doubted the people he was working with. She knew he was already taking great risks to be with her; to expect more wouldn't be right.

She dragged herself up the stairwell of her apartment block, the crumbling concrete still lying loose on the steps no matter how fastidiously Frau Steuler swept them. At the door, she shouted, 'Hello?' Thankfully there was no reply. She couldn't deal with her mother just at that moment.

Miriam threw down her bag and slumped into one of the chairs at the cluttered table. She put her head in her hands and sighed. This whole thing had almost been too much for her. She was grateful at least she could talk to Magda. The two of them had been friends for years. Magda had known about Gerd from the beginning. She had her own boyfriend, so she understood, unlike Miriam's mother. Her friend's advice had been to follow her heart. That was all well and good because Miriam's heart was torn right now; she still really had no idea which way to turn.

***

Gerd Braun felt lighter. All the stresses and strains melted away when he saw her. He would do anything for her and he hated seeing her so troubled by the decision she now had to make. He took comfort from the fact it wasn't him upping the ante; the sudden opportunity with Walther Noltke's tunnel was now forcing the pace.

He'd taken the usual precautions after he'd left Miriam. He thought he'd seen somebody watching them on Alexanderplatz just before they were about to part, but it was so hard to tell. The woman in the red jacket pushing the pram had disappeared quickly, so Gerd didn't worry about it after that. It was nearly dark as he made his way to the checkpoint. His mind was now returning to Heidelberger Strasse and the days of digging in front of them; there was a lot to be done before anybody could even consider escape.

The border guards ushered him through the first gate. If Gerd's mind hadn't been elsewhere, he might have noticed the two men in cheap suits sitting in the Wartburg at the back of the administration building. Perhaps he was so confident in his documents that he didn't perceive the checkpoint to be a threat anymore.

He handed over his passport with the entry visa paper inserted. The officer didn't look at Gerd's passport, nor did he take out the entry visa. Instead he looked back at Gerd, his expression blank and uncaring. 'I'm sorry, sir, there is a problem with your papers. Please step into the office opposite.'

Gerd didn't quite comprehend the words, but he soon understood when he felt a strong arm guiding him.

'*Bitte.*'

One of the men in the cheap suits was at his side, firm and uncompromising. Gerd allowed himself to enter the room; he had little choice. There was only a desk and another man looking out of the window, his back to Gerd.

'Sit down.'

He cautiously took the chair. He could feel himself starting to sweat. He had to remain calm. This had never happened to him before, but it had to others. It wasn't that unusual to be kept waiting at the checkpoint, often to be allowed to eventually pass through without ever knowing the real reason for the hold up.

The door closed behind him and finally a man in a beige raincoat turned towards him. He was of medium height, with sandy coloured, thinning hair. Beads of sweat were apparent above his top lip.

'How was your visit to East Berlin?'

Gerd felt danger. This man was Stasi through and through.

He placed Gerd's passport down on the table, and tapped it lightly, twice. 'These documents are fake. Good quality, but nonetheless fake. Where did you get them?'

Gerd feigned innocence. 'It is my passport…'

'Don't!' The man held up his finger dramatically, then wagged it slightly in warning. 'Permit me to say a few words and then you will understand your position.'

Gerd swallowed hard, his mouth suddenly parched.

'You' – he pointed, dipping his head in mock salute – 'are very good. Difficult to follow, hard to pin down, yet we didn't need to do that. We knew you had to come back to this checkpoint in the end.' There were rules; Gerd had to return before midnight.

The man was watching him intently and Gerd couldn't help squirming in his seat, feeling increasingly uncomfortable. The Stasi man turned and walked back to the window. It was a ploy; the view of a wall with barbed wire and the side of rough-shod apartment blocks wasn't up to much.

A threatening silence ensued, only broken by the roar of a truck engine on its way through the checkpoint. Gerd felt the vibration in his chest.

The Stasi man turned, looking almost apologetic now.

'You're in it up to your neck, Gerd.'

CHAPTER 9

MAY 1962, WEST/EAST BERLIN

Jack had just taken his first gulp of coffee when the buzzer sounded. Tanja bolted for the door in excitement without knowing who was on the other side. Jack expected the postman, only to find Klaus, a present under his arm.

'Grampi!' Tanja squealed, holding her out her arms.

He looked on in bemusement as Klaus thrust the gift into his hands and picked Tanja up.

'And how is my little granddaughter?' Klaus threw her up in the air amidst shrieks of delight. Jack stood aside in shock as Klaus breezed into the apartment.

'Daddy's only just having his breakfast,' Klaus said to Tanja. He always had a put-down for Jack. The beginning between them hadn't exactly been harmonious but, despite some friction, they tended to get on these days.

'Coffee, Klaus?' Jack said.

He nodded. 'Where's Eva?'

'Early shift at the hospital.'

'Grandpa brought something from the airport.' Klaus took the present from Jack and hid it behind his back. Tanja tried to reach behind him, eyes wide in excitement.

'Sometimes you need to be patient, little one.'

Jack rolled his eyes.

Finally, Klaus handed Tanja the gift and she predictably started to claw eagerly at the wrapping paper.

'Probably better Eva's not here anyway,' Klaus said, still focused on his granddaughter.

The thought had crossed Jack's mind that Klaus knew his daughter would be at work, and that's what he'd planned all along.

'Early start?' He handed Klaus some coffee.

There was a squeak as Tanja squeezed the plastic doll in a yellow dress.

Klaus shrugged. 'Same time every morning. Not everybody eats breakfast as late as you, Jack.' He gave him a sly glance, just to let him know it was only a joke. Jack wasn't sure it was. He sat down at the table and Klaus joined him.

'So, how far have you got?'

Jack shook his head, smiling at the man opposite him. Klaus was now in his early fifties, but seemingly not lacking energy. It was easy to see how he'd survived Stalingrad and what came after. His cheeks were weathered, but his eyes shone blue, just like all the Schultzes.

'Hello, Jack. How are you, Jack? How's Eva?'

Klaus laughed, waving him away. 'Come on, there's no need for such formality.'

Jack raised his eyebrows. This was coming from the man who'd only just stopped calling him Kaymer. 'What's the urgency?'

'You know what I'm talking about. He didn't think twice about helping us that night, Jack.'

'It seemed he had little choice to me.'

'I know we helped him with Bernie, and he needed our help, but still…'

Klaus turned his attention back to Tanja who was babbling to her new-found friend.

'How do you even know he still wants to get out?' Jack asked.

'I'm going on what Schwarzer told me. He lost his wife and child a few years back. His parents and brother died during the war. He has nobody over there.' He turned to Jack. 'I feel like I owe him.'

'He took a bullet so his friend could get away, not for you or Eva.'

Klaus shook his head vehemently. 'You're wrong, Jack.' His eyes were on Jack and he felt it. 'Dobrovsky's bullet was meant for me, not Hans Erdmann.' Klaus's heartfelt words settled between them. His view hadn't changed much in the intervening months, but Jack wondered how much he could do. 'So, did you find anything out?'

'Nothing precise at the moment, but maybe there is something.'

'Like what?'

Jack sighed, reluctant to raise hopes. 'A tunnel.'

Klaus's eyes widened momentarily. 'Where?'

He looked at Klaus knowingly. 'All in good time, Klaus.'

Klaus pursed his lips and picked up his coffee cup. 'We've got to get him out, Jack.'

'I agree, and I want to help, but we can't go rushing in there. It's a risky business.'

Klaus scoffed.

Jack looked at him seriously. 'Finding out about a project is one thing, gaining trust is another. Rushing in there like a bull in a china shop doesn't help; I should know.' Klaus looked at him sullenly. 'If you think you can do things any quicker, go ahead. Besides, you probably know the best person to help over there.' Jack flicked his head in the vague direction of East Berlin.

Klaus' face became slightly ponderative. 'Yes, well, I didn't want to involve him unless we really had to.'

***

Gerd felt sick and it wasn't only due to the rank, fetid smell from the bucket in the corner. He heard the latch on the spyhole from the cell door fall back. That was the third time already. They were watching him, watching him sweat, no doubt marking down their observations of his behaviour. At sixteen years old he shouldn't have been sitting in a stinking cell somewhere in the bowels of Hohenschönhausen. Nobody wanted to be there.

He tried to focus his mind. He had always been renowned for thinking on his feet, but the emotional strain of the last few weeks had seemingly turned his mind to jelly. What did they know, exactly? They knew the passport wasn't genuine. They knew his real name, but how did they find out? They were waiting for him at the checkpoint, of that there was little doubt. His instinct told him somebody had been talking.

He had to get out of this place. His one saving grace could be his age. They couldn't keep him for any length of time, especially if Jack started to push his contacts, maybe even the publication he worked for. That would take time, time he didn't feel he had. He was supposed to be back in West Berlin digging the tunnel, the tunnel that would help Miriam, among others, to escape.

He knew that wasn't going to happen now.

***

He woke with a start, the key rattling in the lock. The door swung open.

'Get up!'

Gerd slowly dragged himself to his feet.

'Outside, Prisoner 46! Wait by the door.'

There wasn't a flicker in the face of the guard as he pulled the cell door shut.

'Follow me, Prisoner 46!'

He flashed a look either side of him, quickly taking in eight, maybe ten cell doors, grey paint peeling from them.

'Eyes front!'

They reached some steps and ascended to the next level. Another guard opened the door at the top of the stairs and Gerd was momentarily blinded by the lights. When his eyes adjusted, they were on a long corridor with brown and cream painted walls, a myriad of doors on either side with lights above, some red, some green.

'Wait here, Prisoner 46!'

The guard opened one of the doors and looked inside.

'Inside! Sit down, hands under your thighs!'

Gerd turned to look at the guard, wondering why they were so many barked orders.

'Eyes front!'

He sat down and reluctantly puts his hands under his legs. There was a table opposite him. The window was open, fresh air blowing in. It appeared to be a nice day in the city.

The rest of the room was bare except for a cupboard in the corner and a chair on the other side of the desk. It looked more comfortable than the one he'd been directed to sit on.

Gerd heard the door open behind him and a man, breathing heavily, walked around the desk to face him. He had dark, slicked-back hair and wore a smart jacket, not buttoned up; his portly frame wouldn't allow it. The man placed a buff folder on the table in front of him and sat down. He didn't look at Gerd. He opened the folder, took out a blank piece of paper and placed it to his left, then he took out a typed document and placed it to his right.

Finally, he looked up and smiled sourly. 'I am Weber. I am here to talk to you about the choices you have.'

Gerd thought it best to keep quiet for the time being.

'Four years for the false papers. And that's not all.' Weber shook his head. 'I assume you've heard of Bautzen, Gerd?'

Gerd swallowed hard. He'd heard about it. Most people had. He shrugged all the same. He wasn't about to let Weber intimidate him.

'Ah yes, you're one of the tough guys,' Weber said sarcastically. 'An institution like Bautzen can break a man, even one as resourceful as you.'

He wondered where Weber was going. He hadn't missed the flattery in the last statement.

'But it's not you I'm worried about.' Weber raised his eyebrows, dark bushes like a pair of slugs. Gerd gritted his teeth. 'You're wondering why you are here? How did we find out?'

It was a self-satisfied smile, one Gerd wanted to knock from his face. That said, it was worry, more than anger, that was building in him.

'I like you, Gerd. You're smart; always watching your back, careful in everything you do.'

There was another pause. The only sound in the room was the heavy rasp of Weber's breathing.

'We didn't have to focus on you.'

Weber was enjoying the slow reveal, whilst the dread grew inside Gerd. He felt like he was driving a car; it was out of control and now heading for a full-on collision.

'Miriam told her friend, Gerd. She told her all about you and what the two of you planned.'

There it was. Head-on into the wall. Gerd couldn't help closing his eyes.

'So, we now have you entering the DDR illegally, and more seriously, aiding and abetting *Republikflucht*.'

When Gerd opened his eyes again, he was sure Weber was drooling.

'It's not only you now, tough guy. Do you think she'll cope in prison, Gerd? Hoheneck. Have you heard of that place?'

Somebody once told him the women's prison there was worse than Bautzen. Weber continued to probe at his weakest spot, jabbing at the open wound.

'I'm not sure she'd survive…'

'All right!' Gerd snapped. 'I heard you.'

Weber's dark eyes stared back at him. There was no smile this time, but there didn't need to be; he'd made his point and Gerd had felt it like a knife in his side. His mind felt sharper now, working quickly. 'Have you arrested her?'

'Not yet, but it's planned.' Weber looked at his nails, like he didn't care one way or the other. 'It could be stopped, of course.'

Gerd sighed deeply. 'What do you want?'

'Good, I'm glad you realise the gravity of your situation.'

Gerd wanted to strike out and floor Weber but managed to keep his anger under control. It was about Miriam now.

He stared hard at Weber. 'I asked you what you wanted.'

'Details of the escape organisation you are involved with.'

'I'm not involved with any organisation.'

Weber scoffed. 'Your papers are professional, Gerd. Quality like that doesn't come from a back-street monkey.'

Gerd shrugged. 'I bought them. I needed to get to see Miriam. I'm known in East Berlin. I couldn't exactly use my own passport.'

Weber smiled. 'So, you want to play the game. I have all the time in the world, Gerd.'

'I don't know any escape organisation. I couldn't even give you the name of the person I got the passport from. These people are careful...' He looked directly at Weber. '...for obvious reasons.'

Weber sighed resignedly. 'I thought you might say that.'

This flew in the face of everything Gerd Braun believed in; he was no snitch. He'd not done that when he'd found himself in trouble with the police in the past and he wasn't about to start now.

Weber seemed to be one step ahead. 'This isn't about some stolen cigarettes, Gerd. You're not at the local police station avoiding dropping your mates in it. This is different. You have to be smarter than that.'

Gerd felt fear, but he certainly wasn't about to put anybody in jeopardy.

'Let me make this easier for you.' Weber said. He tapped the papers on his right. 'Here is your confession. It's all here, neatly typed. You can sign this and spend the next ten years at the Republic's pleasure.'

Gerd straightened his shoulders to show Weber the thought didn't faze him.

'Oh, and of course, Miriam will have a confession just like it.'

Gerd felt like a balloon deflating, every ounce of fight draining away.

Weber pushed forward the blank piece of paper on his left. 'Or, I can give you this.'

He dipped into his jacket pocket and pulled out a pen, placing it on the bare sheet.

'You want my grocery list?' Gerd said sarcastically.

'Not quite, Gerd.' Weber nodded slowly as if he were building up to something. 'You will write on this paper in your own hand and sign it on the bottom.'

'Write what?'

'Your agreement to work for me.'

CHAPTER 10

MAY 1962, EAST BERLIN

Hans Erdmann looked over the Spreekanal to the workmen sweeping the concrete podium on Marx-Engels Platz. He'd paraded up and down the huge expanse of concrete so many times, all his men cocking their heads towards the political dignitaries and the Volksarmee top brass. They'd even parked their troop carriers across the square early on the morning of August 13th the previous year, the day Hans and his men had ensured the operation to seal the border ran smoothly. He turned in time to see her walking towards him and couldn't help smiling. It crossed his mind that he'd not thought of the need to get out of East Berlin so much since he'd met Hannah Hirsch.

They greeted each other with a handshake, her grip firm, her eye contact unwavering.

'This is becoming a regular thing, us meeting like this,' Hannah said, turning to look at the view over the square.

'We have important things to discuss, do we not?'

'Ah yes, your meeting with my students. Does this invitation mean you've arrived at a momentous decision?'

He tried to stop himself from smiling and changed the subject. 'The first new government building of the DDR. What do you think?'

They looked towards the building site of the new state council, the place buzzing with activity without much actually having yet taken shape.

'I am sure it will be wonderful when it's finished,' Hannah said. 'But you didn't answer my question.'

Hans had thought a lot about it. Was this woman merely a professor at the university, or did she have another, more sinister, role? Or, indeed, was it just Hans's suspicious mind? Had he become cynical after his own dealings with his chiefs, with Burzin and the KGB? Perhaps Hannah Hirsch was simply the breath of fresh air she seemed to be.

'How would it work?' he asked.

'We've been through this before.'

'Humour me.'

She waited whilst a noisy barge chugged by below them.

'I will introduce the topic of the border with my students. You will say some words about who you are and what you do.'

'I don't work on the border now. I train recruits.'

'Ah, so we can talk about the new measures on conscription, too. What they might expect when they arrive at the barracks, for example.'

'Maybe they don't want to know,' Hans joked.

She turned to face him now, those eyes burrowing deep into him. When she did that he almost felt like he couldn't hide, like he had nowhere to run.

'You were against the sealing of the border, weren't you?'

He was about to protest, but he feared his eyes had already given him away. She placed her hand over his. Hans was shocked at her overfamiliarity, yet he didn't move his hand.

'I already guessed somebody is playing games,' she said. 'I can assure you I am not part of it.' Her voice was firm and even. He wanted to believe her. 'For what it's worth, I wasn't completely in line with it, but I understand why it was done. The country couldn't survive without the people that were leaving: the farmers, doctors, teachers, nurses…'

'I'm not sure everybody agreed with you, Hannah.' He could see the pragmatism in her answer, but for him that wasn't the solution.

She sighed. 'I believe the country, our democratic republic, must be given every chance to work. I have seen the atrocities of fascism, the greed of capitalism; they're not for me. I know it's not all perfect here, far from it, but I firmly believe socialism must be given its head in Germany.'

She let go of his hand and pushed the hair back from her face.

The workmen had finished on the podium and had now started on the unenviable task of the cleaning the square proper.

'I suppose your perspective on history is different. The war, I mean.'

'I know what you mean, and, yes, it might well be. I was liberated by the Russians. You might not feel that, like others in this city, especially the women, but I do.'

He could feel the atmosphere between them. This was their first disagreement. He didn't know what to say to fill the void that had opened up, yet he couldn't help thinking this woman was something remarkable. She was strong and clear in her views, yet calming and alluring at the same time.

'The sealing of the border was harsh, I agree, but if it helps our fledgling country to thrive in the end, it will be the correct decision.'

Hans pursed his lips. 'I cannot agree with that sentiment, but I understand why you feel the way you do.'

'Now, as far as the message to the students is concerned, you of course need…' She tapped his forearm to emphasise her point. '…to toe the party line.'

They both laughed. In his laughter, there was some relief the difference of opinion had passed.

'You tell them of the need to protect our borders from intruders and criminals and do what you have to do.' She raised her eyebrows now. 'I assume if somebody requested this meeting they will be watching.'

He nodded; they would no doubt be watching, someone from the Stasi placed in the audience, but was she part of the ruse, drawing him in with her candidness?

'Is there anything in particular you'd prefer not to touch upon?' she asked.

Here she was, pulling him in again.

'I don't think we should talk about orders to shoot on the border,' Hans said, still watching the workmen push their barrow to the next spot for cleaning.

Hannah was thoughtful. 'Yet you were shot. The students might be curious to know if you had a weapon and were prepared to use it.'

This was sensitive ground, somewhere he didn't want to go. 'They probably will be, but it's not something I'm prepared to talk about.'

She looked at him now, her head on one side. No matter how much he tried to prevent it, he couldn't help smiling.

'What?' she said, giggling in a carefree manner.

'Nothing, it's nothing.' She couldn't see what was going on inside him. This woman was waking him up from a self-imposed emotional slumber.

She touched his hand again. 'It's fine. I will take control if things move in the wrong direction.'

He nodded, feeling the cloak of Hannah's protection, content there, but still wary.

'I wanted to ask you something,' she said.

'It's not like you to ask permission.'

She laughed. 'No, it's not, is it?' She pushed her hair back again. Did he detect a slight nervousness? 'I'm thinking of taking Miriam to the Mügelsee over the holiday weekend. We sometimes go with other families in the apartment block. Why don't you join us for lunch on Sunday?'

***

Gerd Braun had come to a decision. He hadn't arrived at that point easily by any means, but he knew if he was to affect anything, it wouldn't be from a prison cell. He had to think in a much smarter way than that, try to be one step in front of Weber, rather than squeezed in a vice as he felt he had been for the last couple of days.

They came for him very late in the day. He caught sight of the guards' watch – 11:30 pm.

Up on the corridor of the interrogation rooms, a light suddenly flicked from green to red. The guard stopped him and pushed him into a small alcove in the wall. Gerd held his breath on hearing somebody else approaching. There were boot steps and a sliding sound, as if somebody were being dragged. Gerd went to turn.

'Eyes front! Look at the wall!'

Then they were gone. He'd still not seen another prisoner since his arrival.

'Follow me, Prisoner 46!'

Weber was waiting for him this time, slouched behind the desk, hands together, his fingers touching to form an arc, as if he were thinking. There was one typed sheet in front of him.

Gerd sat down, knowing now what he had to do. He tensed as he did, feeling the pain in his ribs. They could have been a lot harder on him. In the end, it had only been a few smacks with a rubber hose, after the initial punch which had left one side of his face swollen. He knew why he'd done it. Weber's smug face, the fact he thought Gerd Braun could ever be a *Spitzel*. Tearing up that piece of paper had been momentarily satisfying.

'How are you finding the Hotel of Eternal Light?' Weber smirked.

'First class,' Gerd said sarcastically.

'Well, you'll need to get used to the regime, Gerd.' He shook his head, perplexed. 'I must admit, I thought you were better than your puerile response of earlier.'

Gerd didn't answer, he just stared his opponent in the eye.

It seemed to unnerve the Stasi man slightly, because he changed the subject quickly. 'Anyway, I have something of interest here which requires my signature.'

He pushed the piece of paper in front of Gerd, who delayed before dipping his eyes to the desk. It was a momentary act of defiance which made no difference to Weber, but made Gerd feel better.

It was an arrest warrant.

'You can see the name at the top,' Weber said almost gleefully.

Gerd wanted to kill the man sitting in front of him, but the typed letters of her name told him that probably wasn't the way forward. He'd thought about little else during his time alone. There was no way Miriam could survive an institution like this.

'Miriam H—'

'I can read!' Gerd snapped.

'Good, because once I sign this, the whole apparatus cranks into action.' Weber leant back leisurely. 'And once it starts…' He opened his hands as if mimicking an explosion, or at least that's how it seemed to Gerd.

'And you're going to tell me how I can prevent that, right?'

'You know how.'

'The piece of paper?'

Weber nodded.

Gerd sighed deeply. He hated himself for what he was about to say, but what choice did he have? 'Let's say I sign it, work for you. How do I know Miriam will be left alone?'

Weber shrugged, but the relaxed image was false; Gerd could see the increasing interest in his eyes. 'You would have my word.'

Gerd scoffed.

'I don't see what choice you have, Gerd. You can trust me or go back to your cell.'

He would never trust a man like Weber.

'So, humour me. I sign. Run me through what happens next.'

'You go back to doing what you do, working for this escape organisation, and you give us information.'

'In return for what?'

'Your freedom. Miriam's continued freedom.'

'It's important I'm left alone, no tails…'

'Of course.' Weber was warming now.

'I will need to see her.'

'Oh, I don't know…'

'You said things have to appear as before. Right?' Gerd was in the game now, like he was telling himself, "Use the same shit on him as he uses on you."

Weber shifted uncomfortably in his seat. 'She'll be watched constantly. Don't even think about doing anything stupid.'

'This is about checking she's all right, that you're keeping your side of the bargain.'

Weber nodded, understanding; this was his way of thinking.

'I want a taste of what you can give me, like the names of the people you work with.'

This would always be the awkward part. Gerd had his plan. His first step was to get out, the rest would follow, if he did it correctly. Weber, meanwhile, was almost falling over himself. 'Girmann? Thieme? You must know these people?'

Gerd shook his head. 'I've heard of them, but they're students. I don't really operate in those circles.'

Weber nodded, then his eyes lit up in anticipation. 'What about the working-class hero, Walther Noltke?'

Gerd swallowed. He knew this moment would come. He knew they were desperate to get Walther. There was a price on his head, especially after all the escapes, but it wasn't only that; Walther was once one of their pinups, an East German champion swimmer who they could parade, but not anymore.

'Yes, I know him.'

CHAPTER 11

MAY 1962, EAST/WEST BERLIN

Miriam Hirsch couldn't help feeling excited. Now she knew it would be this weekend when Gerd came to spirit her through the tunnel to West Berlin, there was a feeling in the pit of her stomach. In her mind, she felt like she hadn't yet made a final decision, but her body was telling her otherwise. All she had to do was wait for the courier's contact, which Gerd had said could come at any time over the weekend, and be ready to leave quickly.

The squeaking of the old apartment door brought Miriam back to reality. Her mother breezed in, dropping bags to the floor.

'Help me put these groceries away, would you, darling?'

Miriam sighed, then reluctantly took the bags into the kitchen and started to take out the items. She shook her head. Some of the carrots were strange shapes and sizes. The apples were small and mostly bruised.

'How was your day, dear?'

'No potatoes,' Miriam said aloud.

'An interesting day, then?' her mother shouted.

'I said "No potatoes"!' Miriam was laughing to herself.

'No, not this time,' was the response.

'Not any time.'

'Not to worry, we'll make do with what we have got. At least we're alive.'

Sometimes Miriam hated her mother's perennial positivity. It seemed to have intensified in the last few weeks. That was in direct contrast to Miriam's mood. She knew she was hard on her mother.

Material things were not her major concern. Her tough past, years spent hiding from the Nazis, had put things in perspective for her.

Her mother joined her in the kitchen and started to put the produce away.

'How was your youth meeting the other night?'

Miriam shrugged. 'You know, dull as usual.'

Her mother stopped, and Miriam instantly knew something was wrong.

'So dull, you didn't bother to attend?'

Miriam sighed. What did it matter anymore? Soon she would be away from all the propaganda and able to do exactly as she pleased.

'I've told you enough times, it's not me anymore. I've... grown out of it.'

'Still no reason to lie to me...'

'Don't!' Miriam held up her hand. There was an edge to her voice, emotion that her mother couldn't fail to miss.

'Miriam, I don't want to force you to do something that you don't want to do. You used to enjoy the FDJ events. What's changed?'

'I'm done with parading and making stupid banners about the Amis.'

Her mother touched her hand, but she pulled it away. Miriam had been trying to tell her for long enough, but she didn't want to listen, only to lecture her. She felt angry, but not really with her mother.

'Okay.' Her mother tried to be placatory. 'Let's not argue anymore. If you say you don't want to go, that's fine. You do know you'll have to give them a reason why and it may not help you when it comes to your choice of university.'

Miriam nodded, feeling sad. She felt the tears pricking the corner of her eyes. 'Don't you see, that's the problem. We have to go to stupid meetings like that, with all the pretence and propaganda, just so we are not excluded from society. It isn't right.'

Seemingly, her mother sensed there was something else because she backed off. 'Let's not talk about it now.' She stopped, then said. 'Is there something else bothering you? Is it about your father?'

Miriam rolled her eyes. Her mother always came back to the same topic when she got upset. It wasn't always about that, and it certainly wasn't at the moment.

Miriam shook her head.

Her mother led her by the hand to the dining table. 'Come and sit down.'

Miriam reluctantly allowed herself to follow. In some ways she wanted to tell her mother everything that was raging in her head, how she felt about Gerd, how she wanted to leave this dreary place in which she lived, but she knew she couldn't. Her mother would only try to talk her out of it. She was good at that.

They were facing each other now. She was giving Miriam that look. The one that made Miriam feel like she could see through her, like she knew everything that was going on.

'It's been a long time since we sat down together…' Miriam went to interrupt, but her mother beat her to it. 'I know, I know. It's my fault, what with my work and all the meetings. Just hear me out.'

Miriam sat quietly, wondering what was coming. Another girl-to-girl chat for the afternoon, no doubt. She had to admit her mother had a way of helping her see things from a different perspective, but recently those talks had become less frequent, and when they happened, less effective. Miriam couldn't help seeing through the façade of the party and its leaders. Her mother had her reasons for supporting them. Miriam didn't share them.

'I was thinking we should go away for a few days. I thought we could spend some time and talk things through. What about the Mügelsee?'

Miriam hadn't expected that. At any normal time, she would have loved the chance to relax by the lakeside, but her face must have said something else.

Her mother laughed. 'Does that sound like such a terrible ordeal?'

'Er… no. I mean, it sounds good. But when, exactly?'

'I thought we'd go this weekend.'

***

It was with enormous relief Gerd Braun entered the checkpoint on Heinrich Heine Strasse. Weber had returned his passport and given him an escort back there. Gerd knew why he'd brought him there personally. That was Weber's message, his way of telling Gerd he belonged to him now.

He'd been forced to write the document in his own hand. How he, Gerd Braun, now "voluntarily" worked for the Stasi. He fought to keep down the bile, but he knew that was his only way out. That was his only way to keep Miriam out of prison. He hoped she could retain her liberty, her innocence. Gerd would get to see her soon enough and pass on what information he needed to. She wouldn't be coming west for a while now, certainly not through the tunnel at Heidelberger Strasse. That would be impossible.

He had every intention of going back to the pub and doing his share of the digging. Before he did, he had somebody to see, somebody he wished he'd shared his problems with two days before, then he might not have been in this mess.

He was grateful to see his scooter in the same place he'd left it. He kicked the machine into life and headed for Schöneberg.

***

Whilst Klaus Schultz was reacquainted with his granddaughter, Jack Kaymer had spent the day in the city probing his contacts for more information. It hadn't exactly been a fruitful experience. He'd been hoping to catch up with Gerd but hadn't seen him since the previous day. It was with a heavy heart that he returned home late in the evening. Thankfully for Jack, Eva's presence had kept Klaus off his back until morning.

However, as soon as Eva left, Klaus was on his case.

'Are we any further on, Jack? Is there any news about this tunnel?'

'Anybody would think you've not come to Berlin to see your family. I've told you, it will take time.'

'Is there something I can do to help it along?'

'Actually, yes there is. I don't understand why you just don't swallow your pride and talk to Burzin. You did it for Eva.'

Klaus turned away as if he'd been struck. 'This is different.'

'How?'

'It just is.'

Jack shook his head, feeling Klaus was trying to skirt the subject.

Klaus sat down at the table. He looked edgy. 'Erdmann worked for Burzin. That's how we met in the first place.'

'And?' Jack motioned with his open arms.

'Well, if he's working for Burzin, he's hardly likely to help him escape to the West, is he?'

Jack shook his head. Klaus wasn't making any sense. 'He did last time. It was Burzin who put the two of you together.'

'But Hans didn't get away in the end, did he?'

'Are you telling me Burzin helped his friend to escape, put him together with you and Eva, and then tipped Dobrovsky off? The man he hates? You're not making any sense, Klaus.'

Jack knew it was more about Klaus's pride. He didn't like asking for anything from anybody, least of all a Russian.

Klaus was grumbling under his breath when the door buzzer sounded. The relief on his face at the interruption didn't go unnoticed.

Standing at the door was a slightly dishevelled-looking Gerd, sporting a purple swelling around his eye.

'You'd better come in,' Jack said.

Gerd stepped through the door and Klaus was smiling. 'Looks like you were talking and you should have been listening.'

Jack rolled his eyes, but Gerd managed a laugh.

'Do you want some breakfast?'

Gerd nodded.

Jack and Klaus joined Gerd at the table as he slumped forlornly into one of the chairs. He looked exhausted, like the usual vitality had been squeezed from him. If Jack thought something wasn't right two days ago, it certainly wasn't now.

'Are you ready to tell me about it now?' Jack asked.

Gerd nodded sullenly.

'Let him have some breakfast first,' Klaus said. Jack turned to Klaus, his eyes narrowing. 'Well, look at the lad. Give him a break.'

Jack felt like he was about to explode. His father-in-law had been here less than twenty-four hours and he'd already had enough of his assuming presence.

'Good idea, Klaus. Why don't you take Tanja out, so Gerd and I can talk?'

Not normally a sensitive soul, Klaus looked taken aback by Jack's suggestion.

Not for the first time in their relationship, Gerd was ready to play peacemaker. He held up his hands. 'Look, there's no reason for Herr Schultz to leave us. In fact,' he paused, staring into his untouched coffee, 'I think I'm going to need him.'

CHAPTER 12

MAY 1962, WEST BERLIN

'I knew there was something wrong, but I didn't think it was this big,' Jack said, genuinely surprised.

Gerd couldn't enjoy the view from Viktoria Park towards Templehof. He felt relieved he had told them everything. He'd told them about the tunnel, about Miriam and his plans for her escape. Worst of all, he'd also told them what he'd signed in Weber's interrogation room, even though it killed his pride to admit it.

'You said the Stasi officer was called Weber?' Jack asked.

Gerd nodded. 'Plenty of weight, dark hair, slimy…'

Jack was nodding. 'It's a good thing you didn't tell him you knew me, or you'd never have got out of there.'

'Really?'

'He was the one who I negotiated Eva's release with. I nearly killed him as well, but that's another story.'

Next to Gerd, Klaus was smirking, his granddaughter in front of him in the pushchair.

'I just signed the form to get out, Jack. I'd never work for those bastards…'

'Er… mind the language, please,' Klaus cautioned, gesturing towards Tanja.

'Sorry, Herr Schultz.'

'I know that, Gerd. It was just like with Eva. You have to go along with what they say. They always have you in that vice, squeezing you dry,' Jack said.

'I don't know what to do next, Jack.' His voice cracked.

'Don't worry, we'll get things sorted out. First of all, you have to go back and help them with the tunnel. Act normal.'

Gerd nodded, feeling his stomach sink again. 'I don't know how I'm going to face them, especially Walther.'

Tanja was straining to get free. Klaus took pity on her, unclipping the harness.

'You didn't tell them anything, so you have nothing to be ashamed of.'

'I only admitted to knowing Walther.'

'I bet that had Weber salivating. If they can snare one of their own who has betrayed them, then it'll be promotions all round.'

'Exactly,' Gerd said. He knew it and that's what somehow made it worse in his mind.

'But to see Miriam again, and keep her free, you'll have to give them something,' Jack warned.

They were at the periphery of the park, close to a simple, dark, wooden cross, a monument to the Workers' Uprising some eight years before. They'd caught up with Klaus, who'd been forced to chase after Tanja. He now had her back in the pushchair.

'He's right, you know,' Klaus said; he was standing staring at the monument.

'About what?' Gerd said.

'You'll have to go back to the tunnel sooner rather than later.'

'I know, but I also have to explain my absence. I should have been there yesterday morning.'

'Tell them you got into a fight and the police kept you overnight,' Klaus said.

'I thought about that, but if it was in West Berlin, they'd know all about it. Word travels fast around here,' Gerd said.

'Tell them it was in the East. A minor disagreement about a deal. It wouldn't be the first time.' Klaus raised an eyebrow.

'It could work,' Jack said. 'In the meantime, we have to think about how to manage Weber.'

Klaus was nodding now. 'Get yourself back to the pub and help with the digging. I'll get in touch with someone who'll know what to do about Weber.'

Gerd felt a wave of gratitude. When he'd decided to head to Jack's place, he had something like this in mind.

'The plan was to stay in the tunnel until it was finished. I can't go back there and then leave again. Whatever you can do needs to actioned before I go back.'

Klaus was deep in thought. 'Makes sense. Sounds like it's urgent then.' He handed the push chair to Jack.

He shrugged at his son-in-law. 'This needs to be done now; you heard the lad.'

'What the...? Where...?' Jack stammered.

'I won't be long,' Klaus said over his shoulder.

***

It was just after lunch when Klaus got back. Gerd was on his feet, expectant. Jack was glad Klaus was here to help Gerd, at least. He was also beginning to understand Klaus might be slightly bored with life in West Germany.

'It's sorted,' Klaus said. 'You don't need to worry.'

Jack thought he'd try and save Gerd any more pain and get to the point. 'Who've you been to see, Klaus?'

'Markus. Well, not exactly see, but I've spoken to him,' Klaus said.

'Markus who?' Gerd asked.

'Markus the spy,' Jack said, none too enthusiastically.

Klaus looked across at Jack. 'Well, we had to do something quickly.'

Jack had been here before with Klaus last year when Eva had been arrested by the Stasi. It was almost like it was a competition between the two of them. Jack had to concede that Klaus had come through then.

'You mean the one that was there at the fence?' Gerd asked.

'The one who was at Stalingrad with Klaus, the one who recruited Ulrich…'

Klaus glared at Jack. It was still a touchy subject even after all this time. Klaus had never fully accepted his son being recruited in that way.

'That's great,' Gerd said. 'Can he help?'

Klaus finally cut the withering look in Jack's direction, turned to Gerd and nodded. 'I told him it was urgent. He seemed interested in the Weber link and the tunnel.'

'Did you have to tell him everything?' Jack said.

'I trust him, Jack. Anyway, at least I've helped the lad,' Klaus snapped, before he turned back to Gerd. 'An hour, back in Viktoria Park, at the big monument next to the waterfall.'

Gerd seemed relieved. 'I can't thank you enough, Herr Schultz.' He picked up his jacket to leave.

'Don't mention it, kid.'

Jack got up to follow.

'Where are you going?' Klaus asked.

'With him.'

Klaus shook his head. 'Markus was very clear. Only Gerd, nobody else.'

CHAPTER 13

MAY 1962, WEST BERLIN

Jack was glad to be free of his father-in-law. He'd forgotten just how painful he could be. The fact he'd been able to help Gerd, and so quickly, had been a blessing. He'd decided to step up his own efforts to help by organising a meeting. It so happened to be at his local bar; chances to go there and have a few beers were rare these days, so he was happy to grab the opportunity whilst he could.

The Leydicke hadn't changed one bit since his last visit. Hausmann was behind the bar as usual.

'My God, look what the cat dragged in!' He threw down his newspaper in shock and started to pour Jack a beer.

Jack nodded. 'Nice to see you, too.'

'Two Amis in one day is too much of a coincidence,' the barman said.

Jack raised an eyebrow quizzically. Hausmann nodded to the corner where Jack's contact sat waiting, doing his worst to look inconspicuous.

'Harry, it's been a while,' Jack said, placing his beer on the small table.

'Jesus, Jack, this place is off the beaten track.'

'It has its upsides.'

'How've you been, buddy?' Jack asked, shaking his hand warmly.

'So-so, Jack. Berlin's okay but it's more my home life that's the problem.' There was a flicker of pain in his face, then he brightened. 'Still, it could be much worse; we could be back in Korea.'

He had aged since those days close to the Chosin reservoir, the pair of them young marines fighting a vain battle to push back the Chinese.

'You look a bit stressed, Harry. What's on your mind?'

'You know, the boss is a pain in the butt.'

'We've all got those,' Jack agreed.

Harry worked for one of the larger American TV stations. He and Jack swapped information from time to time.

'Ricksen is talking about shipping me out of Berlin unless I come up with a big story. He's obsessed with escape tunnels at the moment.'

'Isn't everybody?'

Harry turned, his eyes lit up like a child's at Christmas. 'You know something?'

Jack laughed. 'Relax, Harry, for Christ's sake.'

Harry sat back. 'You're right, Jack.' He shook his head. 'I could do with ten beers, not one. I've got Jackie pushing me for alimony and Ricksen constantly on my case.'

Jack looked around the bar, the wooden floor stained, two of the old regulars playing skat in the opposite corner. His mind mulled Harry's words.

'I suppose if there were a project, it would pay well?'

'Sure, the chequebook is out for the right deal.'

Jack nodded. 'I heard the guy at ABC was throwing the cash around.'

'That's one of the reasons Ricksen is hot under the collar.'

'Well, things can't get any warmer without tanks firing across the wall. There's always something going on. Christ, they're even blowing holes in the wall,' Jack said. 'Brandt was true to his word; the West Berlin police are shooting back.'

Only the day before, Jack had run the story of a teenager who had escaped through the Invaliden cemetery and had been shot crossing the canal. He'd made it to the western bank, but the East German border guards had continued to shoot at the boy. The West Berlin police provided covering fire and one of the East German guards was killed in the shoot-out.

Harry said, 'Well the East Germans made a lot of noise about it. I don't suppose it can go on.'

'It can only escalate things. The State Department won't like it, that's for sure,' Jack said.

'How is Matt?'

Matt Collins, Jack's best friend, worked in the State Department in Berlin.

'I'm going to see him later. It's a while since I caught up with him. He's been busy with Robert Kennedy's visit.'

Jack downed the rest of his pilsner and signalled to Hausmann for another. 'You want one?'

Harry thought about it, seemingly torn. He rubbed his face, as if it were a big decision. 'I'd better not. I've got work to do.'

Jack stopped him from getting up. 'Stay where you are, Harry. Sometimes being too hasty can lose you a lead.' Jack motioned towards the bar for another beer.

Harry was suddenly interested. 'You do know something.'

Jack winked.

'Well, I don't suppose I can afford to turn down an offer like that.'

'No, you can't.'

***

Back at Viktoria Park, the view down over the southern part of the city was impressive, yet the soft trickling of the waterfall did nothing to ease Gerd's nerves. He'd recalled Markus from the night they'd escaped from East Berlin with Klaus and Eva Schultz. He was assured and knew what to do under pressure, and that was exactly what Gerd needed at the moment. He recognised he was out of his depth taking on Weber and the Stasi.

He heard a voice from behind him. 'Meet me at the cross, the memorial for the uprising.'

Gerd went to turn.

'Don't turn around. Ten minutes.'

Gerd waited as long as he could before moving. When he did, there was nobody there. People milled around below the base of the large statue, but he had no way of knowing if any of them was the person who had just directed him. For a fleeting moment, he was worried it might have been one of Weber's men, but then got a grip of his paranoia, and quickly headed off to the indicated place at the edge of the park.

What did Gerd want from these people? Above all else, he was fearful for Miriam; Weber had exploited that fear, pressing him until he had exploded in anger, and then until he signed. He had to get a message to her that this weekend's escape was off. If that were done, he could at least return to the pub and help Walther and the others.

Gerd's eyes were everywhere. Was the old man walking his bedraggled-looking mongrel following him? He stopped and scoured the trees for a moment. Even though the park was quiet, it didn't ease his mind.

He was close to the cross now, where he'd been with Klaus and Jack not two hours before. Gerd turned to his side to see a man in his thirties with blonde hair and sharp eyes.

'You asked for help, Gerd?'

He nodded.

'Let's keep walking.' The man glanced casually to his side. Gerd didn't recognise him, but the mannerisms and voice seemed familiar.

'Now, let's get this straight from the beginning: you are sixteen years old; the BND does not work with contacts who have not yet reached the required age.'

'Er... I didn't say I wanted to work for you,' Gerd managed. Is this what they had in mind?

'It was just a clarification. Now, I'm told you met a man called Weber?'

'In Hohenschönhausen.'

He flicked his eyebrows. 'Nice place, even nicer man.'

It sounded personal. 'You know him?' Gerd asked.

'You could say that.'

They walked on through the trees in silence. On first impressions, he seemed surly and mistrustful, which didn't make Gerd feel any better; after all, his hopes were in this man's hands.

'I understand you are involved with one of the escape groups?' the man finally asked.

Gerd hesitated, not sure exactly what to share.

'Let's be clear, Gerd, if I can help you, and it's by no means certain I can, you will need to tell me everything. If you leave something out, it may well have an impact later. Do you understand?'

Gerd nodded sheepishly. 'I've been working with Walther Noltke, on tunnels, sometimes couriering, messages, passports.'

The man raised his eyebrows. 'Risky business, especially for one so young.'

Gerd shrugged.

'So, how did they catch you at the checkpoint?'

He told the man about Miriam and what the Stasi had said. He told him everything about the meeting with Weber, as well as the plans with the Heidelberger Strasse tunnel.

The man was deep in thought, like he was coming to some decision. So far, Gerd had given him everything. It wasn't in his nature to be so open; he found it didn't pay. He'd shared information that he'd not even told Jack. Had he done the right thing here?

'Okay, Gerd, I will help you.'

There was relief, but Gerd did feel the man was starting to sound like Weber. He nodded nonetheless.

'If you do as I ask, listen to what I say, then we might just get Miriam out of East Berlin.'

Gerd stopped. 'But I didn't ask you…'

'Not yet, you haven't, but in the end, that's what you came to me for. That's why you're doing what you're doing with Noltke. And that's why you signed Weber's papers.'

He'd grasped Gerd's position quickly and had already moved on. Gerd was beginning to feel he was in the hands of a professional. 'Someone will have to warn Miriam it's off…'

'And you'll have to give Weber something when you return.'

Gerd nodded, open-mouthed.

'Like I said, Gerd, you need to do as I say, everything. Also, and this is very important, you must not talk about this with anybody. Jack, Klaus, anybody.'

Gerd was still surprised at the man's sudden commitment to help him. 'Why?' he asked.

'Why shouldn't you tell anybody about this?' the man's eyes narrowed.

'No. Why are you helping me?'

For the first time, the man flashed a smile. As warmth spread across his face, he almost appeared a different person. It was then Gerd recognised the family traits.

'Because, not so many months ago, Gerd, you saved my sister's life, and then you helped her escape over the border.'

CHAPTER 14

MAY 1962, WEST BERLIN

Jack's meeting with Harry O'Donnell had been worthwhile. His instinct told him the information would come in useful when the right project came along. He'd enjoyed a few beers with an old friend in the meantime. Jack had to be back at the apartment soon, even though he wasn't looking forward to returning to Klaus's sniping. He had one other meeting before he went home.

He'd probably drunk enough to be driving around Berlin's streets. Harry hadn't been keen to let him go, once they'd started drinking. Jack had dropped him off at the Eden Saloon in search of more alcohol, in spite of his earlier protestations about having to work. Jack knew his next meeting would be alcohol-free. Matt Collins would be working; due to the time difference with the US, his normal working hours took in the afternoon and evening. He parked the car on Fasanenstrasse and found Matt seated at an outside table at the café of the Hotel Kempinski. He was immaculate as ever, pressed shirt, suave suit, sunglasses. He fit right into that particular part of Charlottenburg.

'Always the best places, Matt,' Jack said.

'One of the perks of the job.' Matt smiled.

'Not sure I can say that.'

Matt laughed. 'How's Eva, Tanja? Sorry we haven't been around for a while; things have been hectic at the office.'

'They're good. Tanja's growing up fast.'

'And what about you, Jack? Any scoops you're going to hit the world with soon?'

Jack tapped his nose. 'You'll have to wait and see.'

The waiter arrived.

'Coffee,' Jack said.

It brought a laugh from Matt. 'Is this the new Jack?'

'Not really. We've got the father-in-law staying with us. I'm liable to say too much if I have more alcohol.'

The waiter left them. 'Another shooting last night. The poor sod took a bullet in the head.'

Jack sighed. 'I can't see it ending, especially now the West Berlin police are standing their ground.'

Matt shook his head. 'Brandt is a hothead.'

'I wouldn't want to be in his shoes, Matt.'

The mayor of West Berlin was in a difficult position as far as Jack was concerned, stuck between an angry population seething about the wall and disinterested western allies. Although he did feel Brandt may have stoked the flames somewhat with his recent comments about the police being there "to protect order in West Berlin, but not to protect the wall".

'I suppose so, but Kennedy's not forgotten the letters Brandt sent him last year. He hates the guy.'

Jack shrugged. 'He speaks up for his people. If he doesn't, who will?'

'It's getting too much, though, Jack. They've been blowing holes in the wall in the last few days. I'd like to know where the plastic explosive comes from.'

Jack had a good idea. He also knew the West Berlin police were involved in these stunts, either directly or indirectly, but he wasn't about to tell Matt that.

'They have to get their frustrations out somehow…'

'It's going too far, Jack. Something bad is going to happen, and when you've got people like Clay in the wings, itching to call up the tanks, then…' Matt ended his sentence with a shrug.

Jack smiled. He knew the general. It wasn't surprising he was so popular in Berlin. They'd even named a street after him. Unsurprisingly, that popularity didn't stretch to the State Department.

Their coffee arrived and Matt seemed to have lost some of his stress. 'You're looking and sounding more like a Berliner every time I see you,' he teased.

'Maybe that's how I feel.' Jack watched as two young, well-dressed women sipped on chilled cocktails.

Matt was stirring the sugar into his espresso a little too well.

'I think it's done,' Jack said.

'What… oh, yeah.' He put down the spoon.

'What's on your mind?'

'Ah, it's nothing really. Things are a bit tense at the office. All these incidents on the border are something we could do without.'

'Is that the State Department talking or Kennedy himself?'

'It's the same thing,' he joked. 'Seriously, there's too much going on. We have to keep a lid on it. There's too much US involvement, Jack.'

'Such as?'

'The TV guys running around waving their chequebooks at the escape groups. It's not… ethical.'

Jack raised his eyebrows. 'Desperate people want to get out. They'll try, whatever the case.'

'But we can't be seen to fuel it…'

'*We?*'

'American companies. We have to stop it.'

'I am still hearing "We",' Jack persisted.

'I keep forgetting you're a Berliner now,' Matt said, not without a hint of bitterness.

'You need to relax a bit, Matt.'

His friend sighed, staring into his coffee. 'Look, all I'm saying is, be careful. If you get involved with one of these projects, it could easily get pulled before it gets started.'

'Pulled? By who?'

'Come on, Jack, don't be naïve. The state is leaning on the big TV companies.'

Jack couldn't help smiling at the irony of it all after his chat with Harry; the two sides of the same tale in one afternoon.

'If this is your way of tapping me for information, Matt, I can't give it to you. I wouldn't, no matter how far back we go.'

'I know, Jack. It's just a friendly warning, that's all. In case you're thinking of getting involved.'

***

Gerd should have known it would have been Jack's brother-in-law, Klaus Schultz's son, who they'd call on for help. Ulrich had been recruited by West German intelligence some years ago. Now, at least, he felt a modicum of relief. He wasn't going to Ulrich Schultz empty-handed, because, as he'd rightly said, Gerd had saved his sister's life the year before at the Teltowkanal, helping her escape through the fence.

He knew Ulrich would deal with the job of notifying Miriam about the change of plans without alerting the Stasi. He hoped she would understand. He knew it must be difficult for her, yet a small delay was better than a stretch in Hohenheck. Now all Gerd had to do was hold it together in front of Walther and the others. As he approached the pub on Heidelberger Strasse, some forty-eight hours later than he should have done, at least part of his plan was in place.

Lemmer, the landlord, only laughed when he saw the bruising on his face. 'Another dodgy deal?'

'Something like that,' Gerd mumbled.

He went through to the back without another word. He opened the cellar doors, which formed part of the floor, and walked down the steps with some trepidation.

The first thing that hit him was the smell. Damp soil, fetid air, moisture; it was better than the air in the cell block at Hohenschönhausen, but not by much.

There was an opening in one of the cellar walls a metre or so in diameter. Peter and Jürgen were laid out on mattresses. Arno was on his hands and knees by the opening, pulling a tub full of soil towards him.

'Where the hell have you been?' he hissed. His eyes were resentful. Gerd had to expect it; the size of the pile of soil in the corner of the cellar told him a lot of the work had been completed in his absence.

'I had some problems the other night.' It was his voice, yet it felt weak. He needed to be more convincing.

Walther popped his head from the opening. 'Ah, you made it then?' At least he was smiling, his face covered in soil, not a bother about him.

'What kind of problem?' Arno persisted.

Gerd had talked this through with Ulrich. He had told him the best cover stories were those closest to the truth.

'I got stopped on the border and taken to the police station. The cops got a bit heavy.'

'Over there?' Arno's eyes were nearly popping out. 'Are you insane? At a time like this and you're playing around in the eastern sector?'

Gerd wasn't without shame, but not in the way Arno thought. 'I'm sorry. I should have been here.'

Arno remained incredulous and turned to Walther, somehow eager for him to share his disgust. The other two were now awake, resting up on their elbows, watching on. All eyes were on Walther.

He looked at Gerd and smiled. 'You never could keep your nose clean, Braun.'

He jumped out of the hole and stretched his back upright. He looked fresh compared to the others. Arno was coughing. Gerd wasn't sure if it was the atmosphere down there or the shock of his sudden reappearance.

Gerd was motionless, awaiting Walther's judgement. He knew he'd already be off the project if it was Arno's decision.

'Well, come on then,' Walther said, handing him a trenching tool, 'Time to earn your place on this team. Arno, take a break, I'll do the removal.'

Gerd dropped some of the provisions he'd brought and pulled off his jacket. At least Walther had backed him in front of the others.

Anxious to make up for lost time, and somewhat relieved, he crawled into the opening. The soil was sandy, rather than heavy. From what he could see, they'd already advanced some ten metres, perhaps more. There were no boards to hold back any falls; this was an improvised job.

Gerd couldn't help hearing Arno sniping at Walther back in the cellar. 'How the hell do we know where's he's been? He could have been talking to anybody.'

He heard Walther growl. 'Enough. I've known him since he was a kid. He's one of us.'

With some relief, Gerd scrambled on down the tunnel.

CHAPTER 15

MAY 1962, EAST BERLIN

Ever since her mother had told of her plans for the weekend, Miriam had been in a panic. The only thing Gerd had asked her to do was to be available, so the courier could give her final instructions to get to the tunnel as quickly as possible. At any other time, she would have loved nothing more than to relax by the water, or even swim in the lake, but this wasn't any normal time. She'd racked her brains to come up with an excuse why she couldn't go.

She'd tried to put up a protest, complaining that she needed to study, but her mother had laughed it off, telling her she needed a break now and again. How the hell could Miriam not be there when Gerd had taken so many risks to get her out? She sighed, shaking her head, staring at the list her mother had left her. This was their apartment's share of what was required for the weekend. Miriam had to admit she would miss the way everybody pulled together to organise these holidays. Families from the same apartment block each brought something from the larger list. Nobody wanted to let the others down and it engendered a spirit of togetherness. She wondered if it would be like that in the West.

The search wasn't helped by the flux in her mind, but she eventually found a hardware shop at the back of the train station. She had to shove on the stiff door, then the squawk on the hinges couldn't fail to announce her entrance. The bearded, old shopkeeper nodded an acknowledgement whilst he served a middle-aged man in overalls; the man stared at her, no doubt wondering what a girl was doing in a place like that.

The shop could have been from another century with its array of wooden boxes filled with bolts, nails and fittings. It smelled of oil and grease, just like her uncle's workshop. She finally found the tent pegs at floor level near the back of the shop. She couldn't see the camping stoves. She turned to look down the line of stacked boxes. A younger man in work clothes was standing near her, intent on his own search. Miriam wasn't sure if he worked there.

'Could you point me in the direction of the camping stoves?' she asked.

The man laughed. 'Sorry, I have no idea. I don't work here.'

'Oh, sorry. I thought...'

'Don't worry about it. Are you planning a trip for the holiday weekend?'

'Something like that,' Miriam said, looking over the man's shoulder towards the front of the shop, wondering when the shopkeeper would finally be able to assist her.

The man moved closer to her. He held a box of nails in his hand and was seemingly searching for another item. 'Gerd said the plan has changed. It won't be this weekend.'

He was looking at her intently now. He was older than her, but not by much, his grey eyes piercing her, imploring her to grasp the meaning of his words. She didn't quite believe what she'd just heard.

'Sorry?'

He looked slightly anxious. 'It's off this weekend. You are to sit tight and wait. Gerd will be in touch soon. Very soon.'

Her jaw dropped slightly. Was this real? How did this man know about Gerd? And what was he doing in a place like this, giving her a message in this way? Why hadn't Gerd himself come to tell her? How did the man know she was here? It was then Miriam realised he must have followed her here. She looked around the shop anxiously.

'One more thing,' he said, his eyes glancing casually to the side. 'Your friend, Magda, be careful what you tell her. Perhaps it's not her, maybe her boyfriend, or a relation of his, but be very careful.'

'What?' she blustered, a little too loudly for the man's liking.

'Please, this is advice directly from Gerd. It's for your own good.' He nodded, eyes wide, to reinforce the point.

Miriam felt indignant, taking advice like this from a stranger, who seemed to know all about her.

Her eyes narrowed in suspicion. 'How do you know Gerd, exactly?'

He looked more comfortable now, like it's a question he expected.

'*Vogue.*'

'What?'

'Your favourite magazine. The first one he sold you.'

The man nodded one last time then headed in the direction of the door. Miriam stood holding the box of tent pegs in a state of mild shock.

CHAPTER 16

JUNE 1962, WEST BERLIN

The work had been constant, but Gerd was more than happy to make up for the time he had missed. Whilst he was occupied with intense, physical work, he felt he could at least push his dirty agreement with Weber out of his mind. Arno hadn't been placated by his efforts; the animosity still bubbled just below the surface. Walther calculated they were now fifteen metres into the tunnel, which meant they were under East German territory. It wouldn't be long before they broke through.

Walther was up ahead at the face, leading from the front. Gerd could only marvel at how fast he dug out the soil, so much so he had difficulty to keep up. The distance they had to pull the extracted soil was now the bottle neck. Gerd's hands were blistered and sore, the rope attached to the plastic tubs doing the damage. The next tub finally reached the cellar, his arms crying out for respite. He sighed in relief, then lifted the container, spilling its contents onto the ever-growing pile they'd already extracted.

He needed a break, or at least his arms did. Grabbing some drinks, he headed back into the tunnel, crawling on his hands and knees towards Walther's position. He could hear his friend's curses and grunts as he toiled. He pulled on Walther's leg rather than shouting; they were so close they could hear the guards patrolling up and down the street, talking to each other, just above their heads. If they could hear the guards then they knew the noises they made could also travel.

Gerd had to yank hard on his friend's leg to attract his attention, such was his focus.

'Take a break, Walther,' Gerd hissed.

Gerd slithered back down the tunnel to a place where there was more space and more air. They'd rigged up a small blower to push air through the tunnel, as close to the face there was little oxygen. The lack of air affected all of them, except Walther. He eventually joined Gerd at a point a few metres from the cellar.

'Don't you ever tire?' Gerd asked.

Walther flashed a smile, his white teeth the only clean thing about him. 'Not until we're done,' he whispered.

Gerd shook his head. 'What do you get from all this?'

'Aside from helping people out?' Walther shrugged. 'A thrill. Excitement.'

'You're strange.'

Walther laughed. 'It has been said before, usually by women.'

Gerd stifled his own laugh.

'It's about getting one over on those bastards up there.' Walther flicked his chin upwards, then leant back and took a long swig from a bottle of apple juice. 'I'm the only one in my family who hasn't done time for them. They've even got my dear old mother locked up and she wouldn't hurt a fly. You can't believe the depths those Stasi scum make people sink to.'

Gerd was grateful Walther couldn't see his expression. 'What finally made you leave?' he asked.

'Many things. Friends and family disappearing from one day to the next. I couldn't stand on parade as the "People's Champion" whilst they were doing what they were doing. What made you go?'

Gerd shrugged. 'We sensed it was coming. All the noise last year was building up to something.'

'Right,' Walther agreed, 'but I had to go before then.'

'So, what was the final straw?'

Walther was quiet for a moment. 'They wanted me to take something to improve my performance.'

'Like what?'

'I don't know exactly. They weren't likely to tell me. But there was no way Walther Noltke was taking drugs. I was already the best.'

Gerd smiled.

'It's typical of their hypocrisy. The bigger the lie the better. You just can't trust anything they say.' He mocked Ulbricht's Saxon dialect, '"Nobody has the intention to build a wall..."' Walther spat to his side contemptuously.

'Will you swim again?'

'Some day, I suppose; I don't know.' He shook his head. 'It's hard to explain. This tunnel business is an itch I have to scratch. I have to keep going with it, exhaust it.'

'Do you think it will ever exhaust you?'

'Never.' The whites of his eyes blazed in the darkness, not an ounce of doubt in his being.

'The only thing that worries me is that they will close us down. They are finding new ways to stop us every day, using detection equipment, people informing on us...'

He continued, 'One day it will stop because people will be too scared of the Stasi, or people on this side will have had enough.'

As if to reinforce Walther's words they heard footsteps above them, then laughter; guards on patrol.

'You might get caught,' Gerd said, the words slipping out before he realised what he'd said.

'Perhaps, or they'll shoot me like they did poor Hans.'

Gerd sensed it was the right moment to find out what had really happened that night, but he didn't want to push. In the end, it seemed Walther wanted to unburden himself.

'It's the only time I haven't been the first to pop my head out. I wouldn't put that responsibility on anybody else's shoulders normally.'

'So what happened that night?'

'He begged me to be the first one through. He was eager to get his sister out. Christ, it was no more than a few cellars along from where we are now.' Walther shook his head. 'No sooner had he put his head out did one of the Stasi shits let loose.' Gerd could feel his friend's fists clenched next to him.

'I dragged him all the way back along the tunnel…' Walther was sobbing quietly now. He grabbed Gerd's hand. 'It should have been me, not him. I should have been the first one out. I got him into this crazy business.'

'That's not right, Walther.' Gerd turned to him. 'We're all in it for our own reasons. Not everyone has exactly the same ones, but nonetheless, we all know the risks, and Hans did, too.'

Walther wiped the back of his hand across his face, trying to regain his composure. 'It only makes the fire burn brighter. I'll never give up whilst there is breath in my body.'

Gerd didn't doubt a word of it.

'Now, we should get back to it.' He tapped Gerd on the knee. 'You will be with that girl of yours by the weekend.'

Walther scuttled off back down the tunnel, leaving Gerd knowing full well that wouldn't be the case.

CHAPTER 17

JUNE 1962, EAST BERLIN

Hannah Hirsch had somehow allayed his worries, soothing him in a way that only Monika, his deceased wife, could ever do. Hans had started to allow himself to believe in her. If she was genuine, what could go wrong during his talk with the students? After all, Hannah knew them all. She'd assured him she would deal with any awkward questions. What was he scared of? He couldn't answer that. He'd concluded it was more about his anger, anger at being put through this ordeal, and certainly at missing out on his bid for freedom.

It was a classic lecture room: banked rows of wooden pews, perhaps twelve rows in three angles arced before him. There were cracks and creaks on the wooden steps as the students filed in. Hans looked up, slightly concerned at first; there were perhaps a hundred bright, young faces looking down on him. Which one among them was not who they seemed to be?

He started with an introduction of his past experience. He didn't mention all of it, not his role in the Battle of Kursk, nor his time as a prisoner of the Russians. He didn't talk about the Workers' Uprising and where he was stationed at that time. But he did talk about his role in the operation to seal the border, what his orders were, what difficulties his men faced. Hannah helped by filling in the background, the party line as to why the operation was necessary in the first place.

By the time all the students were heading out of the room for a short break, Hans felt things had gone well.

Hannah whispered to him as they left the room together, 'I think they like you, Colonel Erdmann, and who can blame them?'

Hans felt a surge of excitement. He was surprised, yet thrilled, by this woman's compliment. He did his best to suppress his feelings.

After the coffee break and Hans's brief words about his new role training conscripts, there was a short time allocated for questions from the audience.

A young man raised his hand. Hannah said, 'Go ahead, Uwe.'

'Could the Comrade Colonel tell us what being in the NVA is like? What is the training and what kind of role could a person be expected to carry out?'

'Life in the NVA is interesting and varied.' Hans answered without hesitation. 'As you've already heard, I have carried out many different tasks in my time. Training consists of sixteen weeks at barracks. This is often tough physically.' There was some laughter around the room, as Hans sensed the students starting to enjoy things. The awkward silence at the beginning had been broken. 'Yet it is necessary, to prepare conscripts for life in the NVA, to rely on your comrades and to be ready for the tasks to be carried out.'

'Thank you, Uwe and Comrade Colonel.' Hannah was linking things nicely. Perhaps she was trying to keep things brief for Hans's sake, but he was enjoying himself now.

A young woman raised her hand and Hannah nodded at her to proceed. Hans noticed Hannah staring intently over to his left.

The girl stood, seeming slightly embarrassed. 'Perhaps I have a difficult question for the Comrade Colonel.'

'I will try to answer honestly,' Hans said.

'It must be difficult to have to shoot at fellow Germans, or even order others to do so. I fully understand why that would be necessary, of course.'

Hannah looked at Hans, knowing this was an area he didn't particularly want to talk about. She went to interrupt, but Hans held up his hand; he felt he could handle this one.

'Shooting at intruders on our borders is the very last resort. There are warnings from signs, intruders are given a verbal warning, and, in the end, our borders have to be protected. As far as giving an order, I wouldn't ask somebody to do what I wouldn't do myself.'

He smiled at the girl, who blushed slightly. 'Thank you, Comrade Colonel.'

Hannah stepped forward now. 'I believe we would all like to thank Colonel Erdmann for coming here today and answering your questions.'

The lecture room suddenly echoed as the students banged their fists on the wooden desks in front of them. Hans beamed, glad it was over, but having nonetheless enjoyed the experience.

As the noise died, a voice was raised to Hans's left.

'Perhaps the Comrade Colonel might tell us about his injuries on the night he was shot at the border…'

'I'm sorry, I don't think I know you…' It was Hannah.

A man slightly older than the students around him was standing in the first row, close to the door. Now Hans understood at whom Hannah had been staring. The man must have sneaked back with the other students at the end of the break.

All the students were turned towards the intruder.

'Perhaps he might tell us how he came to be shot in the *back* on the border that night…'

There were whispers and gasps. Hans stared at the man, knowing he'd been sent by Dobrovsky, or one of his acolytes, specifically to try and embarrass him. This was exactly the reason he felt the whole charade had been organised.

Hannah had now moved to a position between the man and Hans.

'I don't know who you are, young man, but you are uninvited here. This is a private session for students in my year group, and you are clearly not one of those.' Her voice was strong and even, and the man looked uncomfortable under her withering stare. 'And should I find out who you are, you will feel the full force of the university authorities, including…' she stopped, leaning forward, then finally hissed, 'some of my rather influential acquaintances.'

The man's face had coloured. He sheepishly slipped out of the pew and headed for the door.

Hannah turned back towards Hans; their eyes met. Hans sensed a passion in them, an empathy, care, perhaps something even more than that.

CHAPTER 18

JUNE 1962, WEST/EAST BERLIN

It was Friday evening and they were very close to the breakthrough. All of them were alert. Nobody was resting on the mattresses now. They all wanted to be there when they reached the surface. It was what they had been working towards for the last week full of toil. Gerd felt excited, even though he knew Miriam could not escape this time. Whatever his personal feelings, he still felt the anticipation and tension that hung in the air.

Inevitably, it was Walther at the face when they finally hit the concrete flooring of what they hoped was the target property.

Walther's eyes widened. 'You heard that too?' he whispered to Gerd.

Gerd nodded eagerly.

Walther began scraping away at the last pieces of concrete as quietly as possible. His face was one of determination and expectation. Were their calculations correct? What would they find above that final lump of concrete?

Walther took a metal pole in his hand. They couldn't make unnecessary noise, but they had to get through the concrete.

They held their breath.

'Well, here goes nothing!' He thrust the pole up in one sharp movement. Rubble fell onto them, much lighter and drier than the damp soil that had covered them for the last few days. They waited with bated breath, pausing to hear if anybody had been alerted to the noise. With no sound, he thrust the pole upwards again. This time the two of them were forced to turn away as a shower of concrete pieces fell by their feet. Gerd wiped the dust from his eyes to see a small shaft of light. They were through.

Walther poked his head through the gap. He came back down and put a finger to his lips, beckoning Gerd to take a look. Gerd dusted the concrete from his front and gingerly raised his head through the hole. There were boxes stacked immediately around the opening, so it wasn't easy to see too much. Without doubt, they'd landed in a cellar. If it was the correct property was the big question.

'Here!' Walther moved Gerd back as he carefully extended the size of the hole so it was large enough to climb through.

'Okay, I'm going up for a look,' Walther said.

He jumped up and started to move boxes away from the edge to permit good access. The others had gathered close to the breakthrough point. Jürgen and Peter were either side of Gerd, Arno slightly further back down the tunnel. Walther was to be the first one to check things out. Nobody questioned his decision. Only Gerd knew exactly what had happened to Hans; this was the most hazardous moment and Walther Noltke would not let anybody else take the ultimate risk.

Gerd immediately peeked through the gap to see Walther creeping across the cellar. With the boxes now cleared from around him, Gerd could see old cameras and other photography equipment. From first appearance it seemed their calculations had been correct. They'd broken through in the cellar of the photography shop and they'd made good time.

Walther had reached a stairway in the corner of the cellar. As he went to move up the stairs, Gerd saw him reach into the small of his back and pull something out. It was relatively dark, but there was enough light for him to see Walther was holding a gun. Gerd held his breath as he disappeared up the steps; he wondered if the others knew Walther was armed.

Walther had been very clear that nobody was to follow him at this time. At the first sign of any trouble they were to head back down the tunnel to the pub cellar without a moment's hesitation. None of them felt particularly comfortable about that, but Walther had insisted; he'd made all of the others swear their agreement.

All the rest of them could do was wait. Gerd felt the sweat dripping down his back as the floorboards creaked above him. He could understand why Walther had the gun. Of all people, he knew just how much the Stasi wanted to get their hands on him. He'd heard it first hand from Weber.

Gerd heard a noise above him. He popped his head out to see Walther back in the cellar. He ushered him back down, but he seemed calm enough. He jumped down to join them.

A broad smile broke out across his face. It told them what they needed to know. 'We're in the right place,' he said, not without jubilation. 'It's clear.'

There were celebratory punches of the air from the others. The men shook each other's hands and roughly slapped each other on the back. Arno still gave Gerd a wary look, but nonetheless, shook his hand. Seemingly, he'd still not forgiven him.

'Okay, who wants to come and see?'

Arno pushed his way forward. Gerd looked at the other two; as the last man there, he felt it was right to give them first option. Jürgen shook his head and Peter motioned for Gerd to go up. They, at least, recognised the efforts he'd made, doubling the work output of the others, and being the only one showing anywhere near Walther's intensity.

Gerd followed Arno as Walther took the lead. There was no sign of the gun; Walther seemed confident the coast was clear. At the top of the cellar steps there was a storeroom in front to their right, a back door on their immediate right. There were shelves stacked along the back wall of the storeroom, partially obscuring the windows. To their left there was another door which Walther had partially opened. Gerd could see a counter on the other side. This would be the shop front which faced onto the border. After disappearing through the opening, Walther beckoned the two of them through. He motioned for them to keep low, pointing at the window.

Gerd turned to look around him; there were bland photographs and cheap-looking frames hanging on the veneer-panelled walls. There were some films and cameras on the limited shelves, in addition to a couple of advertisements. Gerd did wonder if anybody would miss it if the shop were open or not.

They were now crouched close to the front window. There was an orange-coloured fabric curtain which was partially transparent in the sunlight. Gerd could clearly see the "Y" frame of the barbed wire on top of the breeze block wall. He could even see the sign of the Ehrhardt Brewery atop the pub on the other side of the wall. He shook his head, finding it difficult to believe he was looking at the pub from the other side of the wall. They were in Berlin, *Hauptstadt der DDR* (capital of the GDR). It was exactly where they had hoped to be.

Gerd could feel the adrenalin coursing through him. He couldn't help but smile. Arno's eyes were as wide as a pan top. Walther only flashed a grin. He was calmer; he'd been in this situation before.

Just as Walther motioned that they should return to the cellar, they heard voices outside. Instinctively, they all lay flat on the floor. Gerd turned his head towards the window. The voices were louder now, approaching the shop front. He held his breath, wondering if anybody would come in. From the small gap in the curtain, Gerd saw the carbine of a rifle appear, then a shoulder of a guard passed right in front of the window. Gerd felt like his heart had stopped for that brief second. Arno's face was full of fear.

It seemed to take an age, but the guards finally passed by and they allowed themselves to breathe again. Gerd looked towards Walther. The smile of before had not left his lips. In fact, it was now pronounced.

It was true what they said about him; he really did thrive on the danger.

***

Early the next morning, Walther organised for a fully laden coal truck to pass down Heidelberger Strasse. There were no engineers among them; this was the only test that Walther Noltke believed in. Aside from one or two small falls, the tunnel held. Everything was set. After a week of hard digging, the group went home to shower and inform loved ones of the organisation for that evening's rendezvous. The first escapes would commence that evening and hopefully continue throughout the weekend.

When Walther appeared from the cellar for the first time in a week, Gerd was eating a meal in the back room of the pub. Lemmer the landlord had allowed him to have a shower there.

'What are you still doing here? Don't you have a girl to see?'

Gerd was staring into the fireplace, partially tired from the exertions of the last few days, but there was more to it than that. Now the others had gone off to inform relatives their route to the West was open, the reality of his own situation had struck him. Miriam was going nowhere.

'She's not coming.' It was barely a whisper.

Walther stood still for a moment. It didn't happen often, so Gerd knew he had heard him.

'Ah, the black eye is down to her?' Walther said seriously.

Gerd couldn't help laughing. 'It wasn't that bad.'

'So, what then?'

'She couldn't leave her mother.' It was partially true, but Gerd felt bad enough to believe that was the case. The reality was Gerd felt shocking; he felt terrible Miriam wasn't coming; he felt even worse that he'd signed Weber's papers. Most of all, he hated lying to Walther. He couldn't tell him the truth, even though he desperately felt the need to unburden himself.

Walther sat down in the armchair, forcing a plume of dust into the shaft of sunlight. 'That can't be easy to stomach.'

Gerd looked at him. 'How do you do all this, Walther?'

'Do what?'

'Organise all this. Dig the tunnels, kick everybody up the backside. Work twice as hard as they do…'

'I'm not sure I do…'

Gerd was nodding. 'I've watched you. You never stop when the others are resting. You don't take your break when you should. You're constantly nagging them about security. And for what? Your mother and brother are locked up. You have nothing to gain personally.'

He just looked at the fireplace. 'You're just feeling sorry for yourself. I'm not the person you think I am.'

He was even being humble now. Gerd could only admire the man, more than he did before. It only made him feel worse he'd even mentioned his name to Weber.

'I don't believe that, Walther. I don't understand why.'

He sighed. 'Why do I have the passion I have? Why do I dig like a maniac?'

Gerd laughed. 'Well, yeah.'

'I don't really stop to think about it.'

'And?'

'I suppose I'm a bit weird. A fanatic in everything I do. It's a fault.'

'Not to the people around you. You must see the way they look at you. They idolise you.'

He shrugged. 'It sounds idealistic, like some cheap Hollywood flick if I say it out loud.'

'Try me.'

It was as if he didn't really want to think about it. 'I told you the other night. I cannot abide their hypocrisy. But no matter how much I hate them, and believe me, it's personal between me and Ulbricht…' Gerd couldn't help laughing. '…I think people are free to believe what they want. Don't get me wrong, I know there are people over there who believe in communism; they really do. They believe what Ulbricht is doing is right, or they don't know everything he is doing in their name. That is their prerogative. But what I really hate, detest even, is when people don't have a choice. They are forced to do something, or support something, they don't agree with, or even despise.'

Gerd could see the intensity in his eyes now.

'You might feel bad about the girl,' Walther said, 'but by doing what you've done, you've given numerous people the chance to make that choice, Gerd.'

CHAPTER 19

JUNE 1962, EAST BERLIN

Hans Erdmann wondered if the man had started to lose his mind. There were better places to meet. Berlin enjoyed parkland and open spaces by the acre. Hans knew those places like the back of his hand. Indeed, one of Burzin's places of choice was the Soviet war memorial at Treptow. It didn't happen to be Hans's favourite but at least he kept his feet dry. Hans muttered to himself at the absurdity of it all as he passed through the entrance to the Stadtbad Lichtenberg with a towel and swimming trunks squeezed under his arm. Where would the man think of next?

He emerged from his changing cubicle to be hit by a wave of noise. Part of the pool was being used by a swimming team who were being put through their paces by an excited-looking coach, stopwatch in hand, shouting instructions from the water's edge. If Burzin wanted a quiet *treff* this wasn't the place. Hans peered up at the semi-domed glass roof, checking each of the balconies to see if Burzin was already there. He was still shaking his head as he slid into the water, away from the din of the intensive training session.

Hans knew better than to stand on ceremony. He pushed off into the pool to get some exercise. As he plunged his arms into the water, breathing rhythmically to the side, his mind was on his meeting with Hannah's students and more significantly how it had ended. Hans wasn't surprised somebody had been sent to remind him they were still watching him. Even if Dobrovsky wasn't in Berlin, he was clearly controlling things from a distance. What Hans wanted to know was what Burzin knew, and more importantly, what he intended to do about it.

Hans was enjoying the freedom of the water and he'd covered eight lengths in no time. He couldn't remember the last time he'd been swimming. He did wonder if he would be able to swim at the Mügelsee when he met Hannah for lunch the next day. He couldn't help being hooked. The way she had rounded on the Stasi man in the lecture hall, protecting him, and most of all, that look she had given him. Was it possible she was for real?

As he took a breather at the end of the pool, another swimmer ducked under the rope and joined him in his lane.

'Such a great place to swim, don't you think?' Burzin was next to him. Hans had to admit it was the first time he remembered seeing him without a cigarette hanging from his mouth.

'Not the best place to talk, though,' Hans grumbled.

'On the contrary.' Burzin pushed away from the side, using a rather serene-looking breast stroke. Hans wondered if they were to hold their discussion over a number of lengths. Shaking his head, he ducked under the rope to the adjacent lane and swam fast, as much in impatience as ability. Hans overtook Burzin halfway and was waiting for him when he finally joined him at the other end.

A whistle shrilled next to them and three members of the team dived headlong into the water. Bawled encouragement from teammates waiting their turn to swim almost drowned out Hans's thinking.

'So, you finally met your students?' Burzin said.

'You're surprisingly well informed.'

Burzin wiped the water from his face. 'He had somebody there?'

Hans nodded. 'Somebody wanted to know how I was shot in the back that night.'

Burzin laughed. 'A good question.'

Hans was irked. 'It doesn't bother you that he's still operating here?'

'He has somebody here. So what?'

'You're not going to do anything about it?'

Burzin shrugged. 'I'll put him back in his box, should he pop out. You can't prevent everything. Your trouble is you're too sensitive, Erdmann.'

'Maybe you're a bit too relaxed.' Hans looked across at him. 'Maybe you're even losing your touch, Burzin.'

Burzin responded with a dead stare. 'You called me here to tell me this, or is there something important on your mind?'

The swimmers were heading back towards them now, the next three awaiting the handover touch, straining on their respective blocks.

'How are the arrangements to get me out progressing?' Hans asked.

'I wasn't sure you still wanted to leave,' Burzin said, before pushing himself off for another leisurely length of the pool.

Hans rolled his eyes and took off after him. Again, he passed Burzin and waited, his anger rising.

Burzin arrived in his own time, puffing slightly.

'Of course, I'm bloody sure,' Hans spat.

'I just wondered. I mean, it seems you're quite close to the Hirsch woman now. I thought maybe she'd talked you into returning to the ranks of the righteous.'

Hans's eyes narrowed. He wasn't surprised Burzin was watching him, but a thought did pass through his mind. He wanted to reject it as a paranoid moment, not caring to believe Hannah and Burzin were connected in some way.

'You know my feelings very well, Burzin. They haven't changed, and they never will.'

'In that case, I'm working on it. Don't worry so much, but just remember I'll be in touch when you do get to the other side.'

Hans had thought about that and felt he would deal with it when the time came. In the meantime, he still wanted out. That said, Burzin's instinct was right; Hannah Hirsch had complicated things somewhat.

Hans nodded. 'We can discuss it, but I need something in return.'

Burzin scoffed. 'Apart from safe passage to the West?'

'Yes,' Hans said, looking Burzin directly in the eye. 'I may want to take somebody else with me.

Burzin's eyes widened.

Hans pushed himself off with his legs and swam hard for the other end.

CHAPTER 20

JUNE 1962, EAST/WEST BERLIN

Walther stood waiting by the back door of the photography shop. The first of the escapees were expected at any time. Gerd was inside at the top of the cellar steps with a clear view of Walther. Jürgen waited down in the cellar; he would direct the escapees through the tunnel. Peter waited with other volunteers in the pub cellar in West Berlin. Now the time had arrived, the apprehension had gripped Gerd.

He could even see Walther was excited, restless to get going, to spirit people out of East Berlin under the noses of the border guards. This was where things could go wrong. The operation had reached its critical phase where all the escapees were gathering at designated points around Treptow for final transport. From there it would be walking distance to the back of the shop. The tension was palpable.

Gerd descended to the cellar, where Jürgen was in place on the edge of the opening down to the tunnel. The men exchanged nods and Gerd went back up to watch Walther. They had all seemed to have forgiven his late arrival at the pub, all, that is, except Arno. He was still surly and suspicious. Close to the end of the digging, Arno had suffered a panic attack due to claustrophobia. The lack of air and confined spaces of the tunnel could do that to anybody. When Arno had come around after the attack he'd snapped at Gerd that, 'Some of us have been down here longer than others.' He'd been given the role as lookout above the pub, out in the open air, watching the guards and the shop front directly facing the border.

He checked his watch again. The first batch of escapees was due in the next five minutes. It was a close, humid night. The constant thump of his heart sounding in his ears was the only sound. He wiped the sweat from his brow.

Suddenly, Walther held up his hand in warning. He pulled open the door further, straining his ears. Gerd felt parched, barely able to draw breath. It was slightly early, if it was the first of the escapees, but nobody knew what was happening out there on the streets. Walther pulled the door until it was nearly closed, then shook his head. False alarm.

Gerd breathed again. A trickle of sweat rolled down his back. He peered through the small gap in the door to the front of the shop, the wall side of the building. Everything was quiet and still. He hoped it remained that way. Guards were passing the shop every fifteen minutes. He wondered if it was realistic to shift so many people out from under the noses of the Stasi observing from the windows above and the guards patrolling below. Yet they'd expended so much effort to get this far, digging like moles, bringing families and friends close to the tunnel, they had to try, even though the risks were immense for all concerned.

They'd reached the time the first group should have been there. Walther carefully opened the door and went to creep out into the back yard.

'Walther, no!' Gerd hissed.

He waved away Gerd's protests. It wasn't the time to be deviating from the plan, but Walther was a law unto himself. He thrived on the maximum possible risk.

If there was something wrong, and the Stasi had picked anybody up on the way, escapees or couriers, it was possible the shop itself was now under surveillance. The further they ventured from the mouth of the tunnel, the further they were from their means of escape, their bolthole back to West Berlin and the safety of the pub cellar.

Walther was out of sight and Gerd was getting worried. The first escapees were now five minutes overdue. He was tempted to go out into the yard to see for himself when there was a dull thud from the front of the shop. Maybe his ears were playing tricks on him. He peered through the gap in the door but couldn't see anything. Sweat dripped into his eye and he wiped it away quickly, struggling to concentrate. Then he saw a shadow from the front window. He was sure something moved.

His anxiety deepening by the second, Gerd turned his head towards the back door, willing Walther to return to his post, but there was no sign of him. He had to be sure there was someone at the front of the shop, so he opened the door leading to the shop counter area slowly. He could see more clearly now. There was a shadow, moving slightly. Then he saw someone crouched by the shop doorway. None of the escapees would be brought to the front of the shop in full view of the guards. It could only mean they'd been compromised.

He had to warn Walther. He felt sure they were about to kick the front door in. Why hadn't they had a warning? He checked again, wanting to be sure his eyes weren't deceiving him. Then he saw it, the outline of a rifle. There wasn't a second to lose.

He bounded down the cellar steps and hissed at Jürgen, 'Get back! Now!'

His eyes were full of panic. 'Where's Walther?'

'Just go!'

Gerd looked back up the stairs. He couldn't leave his friend, even though the opening of the tunnel was beckoning him to safety.

Cursing, he shot back up the stairway. He didn't even bother to look in the direction of the front door this time; he just made for the yard. There was a tall gate which was ajar. Gerd pulled on it, cringing at the squawk it made. There was an alleyway, washing lines criss-crossing it to the buildings opposite. Gerd looked one way then the other. There was Walther, crouched at the end, five metres away.

Gerd wanted to shout a warning but that would only attract the guards' attention. He quickly looked around on the ground and found what he was looking for. He picked up the stone and, without hesitation, threw it in Walther's direction.

It struck the wall opposite Walther who whipped around, shock on his face.

Gerd waved at him frantically to come back. Realising something was wrong, Walther started to scramble back towards him. Gerd moved back into the yard and skipped through the back door, waiting for Walther at the top of the steps.

It seemed like an age before he appeared. 'What is it?'

The crash of breaking glass answered Walther's question.

In a split second, Walther was by him at the top of steps and urging him down to the cellar. Gerd didn't need to be told; he was already halfway down when he heard the voices above.

'Halt!'

Gerd could hear Walther behind him as he weaved through the boxes and jumped feet first down the hole. He hit the bottom with a thud and was on his hands and knees, frantically scrambling. He hadn't heard Walther follow him into the tunnel.

Then Gerd heard a shot.

He didn't move, paralysed in shock. He should go; he was no more than five metres into the tunnel and still in East Berlin, but there was still no sign of Walther. Yet he couldn't move until he knew what had happened. Had the Stasi finally caught up with him, making him pay for one daredevil stunt too many?

Gerd had half-turned, but there was no sign of Walther.

He feared the worst.

Then there was another shot. Gerd flinched, but the noise broke his stupor. Then Walther was there behind him, screaming at him.

'Move! Go!'

Gerd was off, scrambling like a man possessed, nails clawing at the soil. Even that was not fast enough for Walther, who had now caught him up and was forcing him through with his wide shoulders. They dragged themselves frantically towards the pub cellar.

He had no idea if anybody was following them or how far they'd come, but Gerd kept pulling, Walther forcing him along. They could be shot at any moment; there wasn't exactly anywhere to hide. Gerd didn't want to die here.

He felt his arms tiring, the lack of air and all the effort making him feel light-headed. Walther wasn't giving up. 'Come on, we're nearly there. Don't stop now!'

Gerd felt sick, like he couldn't move any more, but forced himself on. Suddenly, there were arms pulling him through, dragging him out of the tunnel.

He fell in a bundle onto the floor of the pub cellar, Walther following hard on his heels. Gerd was on his hands and knees retching, not even enough breath to be grateful they'd made it out.

He could hear Walther laughing manically next to him.

Walther clapped him hard on the back which only made him cough more, his eyes watering uncontrollably.

'We made it! The bastards didn't get us!'

Slowly Gerd came round, his eyes gradually focusing on those around him. Jürgen and Peter looked distraught.

Then he saw Arno. He was seething, his eyes only on Gerd.

CHAPTER 21

JUNE 1962, EAST BERLIN

Miriam Hirsch sat in a *Strandkorb*, shielded from the warm sun, the sand of Rahnsdorf beach trickling between her toes. The lapping waters of the Mügelsee shimmered as children paddled in the water. There were shrieks of laughter as a game of volleyball ensued to her left. She should have been relaxed, loving her time here, but there was no way she could settle. Her heart just wasn't in it. All she could do was think about Gerd. What had happened for him to suddenly call off the escape attempt? And why did he need to send somebody else to give her the news? Why couldn't he come, which in the end, was all she really wanted? She shuddered, not wanting to believe this was his way of abandoning her to life alone in East Berlin.

She wondered how the man in the hardware shop could know Gerd. Her mind panicked and thought for an instant it may have been an operative from State Security. She'd heard they played tricks like that, even though she hadn't personally come across anything like it before. How had he known about Magda? She'd been racking her brains, trying to think what she'd told her. Had Magda said something to somebody about their plans? She didn't want to believe the man. Then he'd mentioned the magazine, *Vogue*. They were the very magazines Gerd used to bring her. Miriam recalled the glamorous Tania Mallet, the English model, wearing stylish trouser suits and pouting as she smoked. The life looked very different to hers and the women she saw every day. The man had been sent by Gerd; on that, she was finally settled.

Her mother couldn't fail to see her torment. She'd tried to have the discussion with her she'd promised, but Miriam had resisted, making excuses about a headache. She was past her mother's pep talks. This was serious now. She didn't want to be here. She wanted out of "Berlin – Hauptstadt der DDR", as they so patronisingly called it. The others had tried with her too, asking her to join the volleyball match, to go for a swim, or even her favourite, hiking along the lake. She'd remembered swimming naked on the Kleiner Mügelsee when the group was younger; all that seemed so frivolous now.

Normally her mother would have tried harder with her, but Miriam could see even her thoughts were elsewhere. She had noticed her happiness, her change in overall mood. This was the day she had invited "her friend" to the picnic on the beach and everything had to be just so. All the food had to be laid, the blanket smooth, even Miriam had been told by her mother to "smile for once". Before he'd even arrived, without seeing her mother with the man, Miriam knew something was changing. Maybe it was a good thing there could be someone in her life, somebody she could rely on; Miriam wasn't planning on being around much longer.

***

Hans hadn't known why he'd said it. He'd not thought about taking others across the border with him before that time, not consciously at least. The more he thought about it, the more he thought he must have been crazy to believe it could happen. In all the meetings he'd had with Hannah, she'd always appeared happy in East Berlin. Furthermore, she'd only ever espoused government policy and had certainly voiced a mistrust of the capitalist world. Why on earth would he think she would give all that up and flee with him to the West? Then there was her daughter to consider. Hans shook his head at his stupidity. This wasn't just about him. As he sat on the tram up to Friedrichshagen with all of the day trippers, he knew the woman had got under his skin. They hadn't even been intimate, and he had no idea if his feelings for her were reciprocated.

Most of the people got off the tram at Friedrichshagen, heading off in the direction of the Spreetunnel and no doubt some liquid refreshment at the bars by the lake. Hans stayed on to Rahnsdorf, already steeling himself to be more cautious. He couldn't afford to lose his emotional armour. He could feel the effect Hannah was having on him and he was fearful. Could he trust her? Was she part of it all? Perhaps it wasn't about that. Maybe he was scared because it was the first time he'd allowed this to happen since Monika. In the circumstances, it was the last thing he had expected.

He got off the tram. It wasn't far to the beach, and before long he could see the low, white and aqua blue painted building which announced "Strandbad Müggelsee". No matter what he'd told himself, he couldn't help feeling nervous as he paid a small fee to access the beach. The place was teeming with life. Hundreds of striped *Strandkörbe* lined the sand, and there didn't seem to be space to move, let alone play the many different games which were going on. He wondered how long it would take to find Hannah among the throng.

He needn't have worried. He spotted her waving him over. She even walked towards him and met him at the bottom of the steps down to the beach. For the first time, she greeted him with a kiss on the cheek, taking Hans by surprise.

'Come and meet everybody,' she said, full of energy.

Hans's nerves had calmed slightly, elated at her warm welcome. She'd been looking out for him, meeting him away from the others to put him at ease.

'Everybody, meet Hans Erdmann... he's a Colonel in the NVA,' she said, smiling knowingly at him. Did he detect a hint of pride in her voice?

There were a group of maybe twenty people. It was too large a group for formal introductions. Most waved and said hello, but Hannah was already looking around. 'Where is Miriam?' she said, half to herself. 'Ah, there she is.'

Hans turned to see a teenage girl with long, dark hair, reclined on a *Strandkorb*. She was looking across at them rather sulkily, kicking her feet in the sand.

'Miriam, there is somebody I would like you to meet.' The girl didn't move from her relaxed position. 'Er, when you're ready to join us, young lady.' Miriam rolled her eyes, then got up rather huffily. 'Miriam, this is Hans. Hans, my daughter.'

'Pleased to meet you, Miriam.' Hans held out his hand. The girl took it, her eyes looking him up and down.

'Likewise,' she said, distant, yet seemingly intrigued.

'Hans is a Colonel in the Volksarmee,' Hannah added.

Hans thought he detected a flash of panic in Miriam's eyes before she smiled.

'I think I'll go for a swim, Mum,' Miriam said quickly. 'It was nice to meet you, Hans.'

She stripped off to her bathing suit and then headed towards the waterside.

'Don't go too far; it's not exactly warm in there,' Hannah called out.

'I'll be fine,' Miriam shouted over her shoulder.

Hannah shook her head. 'I don't know where that girl's mind is these days. I brought her to try and get close to her again, but all she's done it brood in a corner. I'm sorry if she appeared rude; it's not normally like her.'

'It's fine,' Hans said. 'It's not always easy for a grown-up child to meet...' He stopped himself from saying more, feeling foolish.

Hannah smiled that charming smile. 'To meet who, Hans?'

He felt his cheeks colour. 'Well, I just mean it's not an easy age for girls. A lot going on inside.'

'Quite.' Hannah was still smirking, seemingly teasing him in his moment of difficulty.

'I brought some beer and some smoked sausage,' Hans said, quickly changing the subject, holding up a bag.

'All welcome. Why don't you grab two of the beers and leave the rest with the others?'

She looked at him, her head on one side. 'Would you care to share a *Strandkorb* with me, Hans Erdmann?'

CHAPTER 22

JUNE 1962, WEST BERLIN

The room behind the bar was deathly quiet. Lemmer had closed the adjoining door and left them to the recriminations. The feeling of despair that many of their friends and family were still stuck in East Berlin, some now even in Stasi custody, hung above them like a black cloud of depression. They had all suffered. The fallout from their broken venture had been hard to accept and even more difficult to understand.

The relief they'd felt at escaping the border guards was short-lived, quickly replaced by the frustration of seeing all their hard work come to nothing. Walther Noltke sat cross-legged in front of the fireplace, squeezing his empty bottle of apple juice. His knuckles were white.

'They arrested two of our couriers and rounded up fifteen people in total,' he said sullenly.

'My sister among them,' Peter said.

'They took my brother, too,' Jürgen muttered, barely able to believe it.

Arno's relations seemed not to have been affected by the round-up, at least not yet. He still seemed the one among the group with anger to expel. 'I want to know how this happened, how they knew.'

'I hate to say it, but it looks like we have a leak.' Walther said it like it cut him in two.

Gerd hadn't said a word. He didn't really feel like talking. He was relieved they'd made it back through the tunnel; it had been a close-run thing. The newspapers in the East were full of glee at a foiled escape attempt, in which it seemed the "bandits" had been armed and had fired on the border guards. Walther hadn't said anything about the gun, but Gerd suspected he loosed off a couple of shots to buy them time to get back into the tunnel and away to the pub cellar. He was grateful he had.

'I agree,' Arno said, standing with arms folded across his considerable front. 'And I know where the leak came from.'

Everyone in the room looked at him; even Gerd raised his eyes from the worn carpet.

'I think it's time you told us what really happened. Why you were really late in getting back here.' His venom was aimed directly at Gerd.

Gerd flashed a look in Walther's direction.

He interceded on Gerd's behalf. 'I know you're angry, Arno; we all are, but…'

'No, Walther. We don't really know what happened and I don't believe his story for one minute…'

'You think I'm a *Spitzel*?' Gerd said. He was only grateful the leak was nothing to do with him, but deep down, he couldn't help feeling guilty.

'Come on, Arno, you surely don't believe it… What exactly are you saying?' Walther said.

'Ever since he,' Arno stabbed a finger towards Gerd, 'came back here, everything has gone wrong. They knew who the couriers were. They knew the meeting points; they even knew where the tunnel was located.'

'Now, hold on a minute.' Gerd was on his feet. 'I had no idea about the courier arrangements.'

Walther nodded. 'It's right. He didn't know anything.'

Whatever Walther had said, Gerd sensed Jürgen and Peter staring at him, like he had something to explain.

'Yet they knew where to look for the tunnel,' Arno said.

Walther wasn't listening, but Gerd could tell the others were. Arno was getting to them. He had to defend himself.

'I never left this pub after we finished the tunnel,' Gerd said. 'How the hell could I have told anybody anything?' Now he was glad he'd followed Ulrich's advice and stayed where he was.

All eyes were still on Gerd. He felt his mouth going dry. Even Walther was looking at him now. He had a feeling the tide was turning against him, and even though he knew he had done nothing, the guilt of his agreement with Weber was hanging over him, preventing him from being convincing in his argument.

'It's convenient you decided not to leave the pub. It's also convenient your girl decided not to escape with the others. Perhaps you knew what was going to happen.'

'And who was stationed at the front of the pub? Where was the warning?' Gerd shouted, feeling increasingly desperate.

'You're deflecting the issue. We want to know what happened when you were arrested. People just don't walk free from an East German police station after a fight, especially not someone holding a West German passport.'

Gerd hesitated, feeling the onus on him to explain. 'I told you, I got into a fight.'

'With who?' Arno's voice was high-pitched, accusatory.

'Somebody I was doing a deal with.'

'Who, Gerd?'

'Look, what the hell is this? I dug that tunnel with all of you. Why am I under suspicion?'

'Because you're the one who disappeared. You're the one who ended up in an East Berlin cell, and then miraculously reappeared, free as a bird. It doesn't happen, Braun.'

Gerd's jaw flapped open. That second's delay made him feel doomed. Normally he would have been ready to defend himself. He looked around the room and felt the mistrust. The eyes of suspicion that had only belonged to Arno when he first arrived back at the pub had spread to those of the others, including, for the first time, Walther Noltke's.

CHAPTER 23

JUNE 1962, EAST BERLIN

She waded out into the cool water. Even though Miriam was in one of her favourite places, she couldn't help feeling things were closing in on her. She felt she had to get away now, yet how long would it be before Gerd was in contact with her again? How long would it be before he had the next escape plan in place?

She missed him terribly. Even those stolen moments, creeping around in secret, lying to her mother about where she was, were at least something. They were something she could look forward to and cherish, until they could be finally be together properly. As it was now, it seemed she would be contacted by somebody else. What had changed?

The water lapped up to her waist, taking her breath away as it touched her stomach. She was still thinking about the man's warning about Magda. She had told her about Gerd, about their escape plans, but only because she knew she wouldn't say anything. She steeled herself then pushed herself off into the water. After getting over the initial shock, it was invigorating. She spun around to look back at the beach. She tried to pick out her mother amongst the group from the apartment block but couldn't see her. She shielded the sun from her eyes to scan the beach area.

She was used to the water now. She felt more relaxed, her thinking calming a little. She watched as a boy her age raced his father through the water close to her. She had to be patient and wait for Gerd, even though it was difficult. She had to be tougher, more resilient to the ups and downs. It would be worth waiting for in the end.

Then she spotted them, sitting together in the *Strandkorb*. They were laughing, seemingly happy together.

She was surprised her mother was dating a colonel in the Volksarmee. It all fell into place, at least; the reason her mother had been so chirpy recently. Miriam felt this man and her mother had grown close. She was usually so anti-war that Miriam found it difficult to understand why she would choose somebody in the armed forces. That wasn't the worst of it. Knowing what was going on in her head, knowing that she wanted to escape from East Berlin, Miriam couldn't help wondering who this man really was. Was she being paranoid? Here was her mother, introducing her to someone who was an integral part, and defender, of the state she had ultimately rejected.

Her mother stole a look around her, then she leant over and kissed the Volksarmee colonel.

***

Hans found it difficult to find the resolve he sought. Hannah was forcing the pace and he wasn't in control of it. She was the one kissing him on the cheek, taking him away from the others to sit together. Even if he felt the need to go slowly, remain cool, he wasn't able to prevent his feelings. Normally he could do that, but not with Hannah Hirsch.

They sat close together, enjoying the sunshine. Hans's mind couldn't help returning to the meeting with Hannah's students. He had to know if she was genuine.

'Did you manage to identify the man in the lecture hall?'

Hannah had reclined her chair. 'Not yet, but I will.' She sounded determined. 'I know people who will know.'

She was so certain.

'So, what do you think is wrong with Miriam?' he asked.

'There's something on her mind. She hasn't opened up yet, but she will.'

'Maybe she's just growing up,' Hans suggested.

'No, I know Miriam. It's something more than that.'

'Really?'

Hannah looked at him, as if she were thinking about sharing something with him. 'She met a boy – I should say a young man – from the West. Not a great influence, I'm afraid.'

'Oh.' Hans hadn't expected that. He felt certain Hannah Hirsch would never allow such an association.

'He's got into her head.'

'He still sees her?' Hans meant because of the wall.

'She says not, but I'm not sure I believe her.'

Hans raised an eyebrow.

'I found some magazines, Western nonsense. Her head has been turned by the glamour, allured by the bright lights.'

Hans wondered for a moment, then said. 'You don't think…?'

'What? That she's planning to run away with him?'

Hans shrugged, 'Well, do you?'

'Don't be absurd, Hans. She'd have to… well, escape over the border.' She shook her head dismissively, but Hans hadn't missed the concern in her face. 'I'd like to think there was more to keep her here.'

This wasn't what Hans had expected. Was it a softening-up tactic to make her seem more real? It was very clever, if that was the case. He briefly wondered if his conversation with Burzin hadn't been so far-fetched after all.

They were silent for a while. Hans was coming to the conclusion nobody could be that good, involving her daughter in that way. He took in the scene around him and found himself relaxing. He reclined his seat to be next to hers. Hannah was looking at him intently. He could feel something inside him again, really wanting to take hold of her.

'So, now you're here, Hans Erdmann, what are we to do?'

He felt excitement in his stomach, something he hadn't felt for years. He wanted to reach out and touch her.

'Perhaps this isn't the place?'

'Probably not, but at least I think it's time we went out for dinner, don't you?' Hannah raised her eyebrows.

He smiled. Inside he was more than smiling. Maybe he'd not misjudged things after all.

'Don't be afraid, Hans Erdmann. I won't hurt you.'

She reached out towards him and kissed him softly on the lips.

CHAPTER 24

JUNE 1962, WEST/EAST BERLIN

Gerd left the pub, holding back tears. When Arno had accused him, they'd all stood by, only Walter defending him for a while, then even he joined the stony silence. He had run out of the pub. He couldn't give them the answer they wanted to hear, the answer that made any sense. That was because of the guilt, the guilt of his dirty deal with Weber. He knew that's why he couldn't think straight to defend himself from the attack. He understood people were angry – he was as well – but this mess wasn't his doing. He'd had to get out, feigning an anger that wasn't really genuine. It hurt even more that nobody had stopped him from leaving, not even Walther.

He felt betrayed. He had expected Walther to defend him more fervently, just like he had when he first arrived back at the pub, but there was nothing. The worst thing was that they had an informer among their ranks and they were looking in the wrong place. Gerd had never felt as bad as this. In all the years he'd been up to no good, nobody had ever called him a *Spitzel*. He'd dealt with some unsavoury characters, too, but everybody who had dealt with Gerd Braun knew he wasn't that.

He kicked the moped into life, wondering what to do next. He felt now he would never get Miriam out. His so-called friends had shunned him, those who he'd been working tirelessly with, not only on this project, but over the past few months, were against him. The people who he had helped, the organisation he had hoped would bring Miriam out, had been infiltrated. That route now appeared closed. Gerd was ever more reliant on Ulrich Schultz and the BND.

He tried to shake the negative thoughts from his mind. At the moment he felt low, but he would never be in a position to be forced into Weber's hands to get what he wanted; that would never happen. He knew he had to go back to Ulrich and update him, but in the meantime, he felt like he needed a friend.

He headed back towards Schöneberg.

***

As she emerged from the water, something struck Miriam: a moment of realisation, one so horrible she felt sick. She didn't know why it had come then – maybe it was the young boy with his father in the sea – but it had come, and she only wished it were not true. How could she have been so stupid? Magda's boyfriend Horst was a nice boy. Miriam had met him before, many times. The last time was when he had offered her a lift home with his father from the FDJ meeting. She'd not even thought about it then. Why should it matter to somebody like Miriam? She had never done anything wrong before. But Horst's father had worn a uniform. Magda had even mentioned it once before in passing. He was State Security. The Stasi, some people called them. She closed her eyes. Could it be?

She felt like falling to the sand and weeping. What had happened to Gerd? Had he been arrested because of what she'd said? But if he was in prison, how did he get the message to her? She looked around her. Was she being watched now? She felt hysterical. Then she looked at her mother with that man. She felt a jolt of fear. Who was he really? Was he really a colonel in the Volksarmee, or had he been sent to keep an eye on her?

She reached her towel and dried herself off quickly. She got dressed in a trance. Surely her mother would know if this man wasn't for real. Miriam felt distraught. She just needed to get away from the beach.

She started to walk away, but her mother had spotted her and was heading her off.

'We're going to have some lunch, darling. Are you going to join us?'

'I'm not hungry.' She couldn't hide the anger in her voice, even though she knew she needed to control it, until she could work out what was going on.

'What's the matter, Miriam?'

'Nothing.' She could feel the tears forming in her eyes.

'Come on, what is it?'

'Who is that man?' Miriam snapped.

'I told you…'

'Are you sure?'

Her mother appeared shocked. 'Look, Miriam, are you all right?'

'No, I'm not all right.' She felt herself losing it now. 'You're kissing a man in public who you barely know.' Her voice was raised, and she had attracted the attention of people around them. Her mother seemed embarrassed, which Miriam had never seen before.

'Miriam, I don't think this is the place…'

'Not the place? We came here to talk, yet all you can do it canoodle with a man you don't even know.'

Miriam couldn't help it. All the emotion of the last few months, and then her sudden realisation had tipped her over the edge. She knew it wasn't fair on her mother, and that she was being unreasonable, but she couldn't help it.

Her mother was lost for words. The people around them stared, transfixed by their confrontation.

The tears rolled down her cheeks as she grabbed her bag and stormed towards the exit.

'Miriam, please!'

'Just leave me alone!'

CHAPTER 25

JUNE 1962, WEST BERLIN

The bad atmosphere at the apartment remained, hanging like the stench from a pair of week-old, soiled socks. Klaus was still there, and Jack was still praying for the day he packed his bags and headed back to West Germany. Jack felt bad for Tanja as she didn't get to see her grandfather that often, but having him around was only increasing Jack's frustration. He felt like he was getting to a point where he may be able to help Hans Erdmann with something concrete, but Klaus's constant nagging, and undermining him, didn't move things along any quicker. In fact, he wondered exactly what Klaus himself was doing to help Erdmann.

Thankfully, as the weather was so good, Klaus had taken Tanja and Eva out for the day. Jack breathed out audibly when they left. At least it gave him some time to get on with some work for once.

The door buzzer sounded, and Jack's heart sank at the interruption. As he opened the door, Gerd stormed past him, his face like thunder. Jack thought he detected a slight reddening of his eyes.

'Jack, how are you doing?' Jack said, ironically.

Gerd turned in the middle of the lounge area to face him. He could see the pain in his friend's face. Gerd sat down and put his head in his hands.

Fighting back the tears, he said, 'They think I'm a snitch, Jack.'

Even after his brief stay in Hohenschönhausen, Gerd didn't look this bad.

Jack sat down next to him. 'What happened?'

Gerd's head slumped on Jack's shoulder. He put his arm around him and Gerd started to cry. His sobs were heartfelt, and Jack couldn't help thinking there was still a child in there. Gerd was one who had been made to grow up too quickly, take on too much responsibility, trading for food so his younger siblings could eat. He'd never seen him like this before; the usual fierce independence seemed to have melted from him. Jack could only feel sympathy. As much as he loved Berlin, if you let it, the city could burn you.

After some time, he calmed down. Jack got him a hot drink and finally, Gerd was ready to talk.

Jack was trying to fathom what had happened. 'How could this be your doing? How could they think that? Unless…'

'Unless what?'

'Weber's men followed you.'

Gerd shook his head. 'I worked through everything with Ul…' He stopped himself, looking at Jack with wide eyes as if he'd said too much. 'I was very careful. Anyway, that doesn't explain how they knew where the couriers would meet the families.' He shook his head. 'They knew everything.'

Jack ignored Gerd's mid-sentence slip. He'd already suspected Markus's contact in Berlin was Ulrich Schultz, but it wasn't the time.

'You said neither you nor Walther left the pub after the tunnel was finished?'

'That's right. The others went to tell their families,' Gerd said. 'You should have seen them all, Jack. None of them would even look at me when Arno was accusing me.'

'What did you say to defend yourself?'

'I tried, Jack, believe me. Arno kept asking me what had happened when I was arrested. Why I was late back. I couldn't think straight.'

'I don't understand why they can't see it couldn't be you.'

'I wasn't very convincing.' Gerd shook his head. 'I should never have signed that piece of paper.'

'Rubbish. You did what you had to do, and even then, you told them nothing they didn't already know.'

'But don't you see? It made me look guilty, even if it wasn't the case. I'm not a good liar.' Jack couldn't help raising his eyebrows. Gerd laughed. 'Well, it depends if I'm selling something.'

'That's better, at least there's a smile.' He ruffled his friend's hair.

Jack could understand why Gerd felt like he did. This was about honour for him, respect among his contacts in the city, *not all of them one would be proud to call friends*, Jack thought, but reputation was everything to Gerd; Jack liked that in him. Only Gerd's pride was clouding the real issue. Somehow, information had leaked out from the group in the tunnel, or from somebody else in Walther Noltke's organisation.

'How many people knew about the couriers and the meeting places?'

'I have no idea,' Gerd said. 'Walther, for sure. Of the others, they would have known for their respective families. In the wider group, I don't know.'

'So, the leak could be anywhere?'

Gerd shrugged, 'I suppose so.'

'The one thing we know for sure is that it wasn't you.'

'That's not what they believe.'

Jack's mind whirled with all the possibilities. He knew how the Stasi could get to people, coerce them over loved ones' well-being, greed, things they want to hide. They'd done that to Gerd. How many others within the network had suffered the same fate?

'You said you were nearly caught by the guards who came in the front of the shop?'

'Yes, Walther and me.'

'The shop front looks onto the wall and can be seen from the other side, our side, of the wall?'

Gerd nodded.

'Then why didn't you post a lookout in the apartments above the pub?'

'We did.'

'So why didn't you get a warning the guards were outside the shop?'

'I mentioned this, but the fight wasn't in me, Jack.' Gerd shrugged his shoulders. 'Maybe they didn't have time to warn us.'

Jack looked sceptical. 'As a matter of interest, who was the lookout?'

'Arno.'

CHAPTER 26

JUNE 1962, EAST/WEST BERLIN

Miriam didn't care where she went; she just had to get away, away from other people, away from her mother. She had boarded a tram, intending to head back into the city. She sat on the wooden bench in despair. What had she done to poor Gerd? She hated herself for telling Magda about their plans and she was angry with Magda for talking to her boyfriend about it. It was the only explanation for what had happened and why the man in the hardware shop had warned her. But in the end, it was only because of her. She'd been so naïve and foolish. The whole thing could have been avoided if she'd kept her mouth tight shut.

She felt completely alone, like she had nobody to talk to now, no one with whom to share her worries. Miriam closed her eyes as she thought about how she'd behaved at the beach. She'd been awful to her mother in her moment of realisation, in that irrational moment when she'd feared exactly who Hans Erdmann might really be. It seemed unlikely to her the Stasi would be so obvious if they were following her. She shot a glance over her shoulder, wondering if they were watching her now. The tram was just a sea of anonymous faces; an old man reading a worn book, a woman fussing over her children. How would she recognise them anyway?

The tram stopped at Friedrichshagen and Miriam decided to get off. Perhaps running back into Berlin wasn't the right thing to do. She headed down to the waterfront where the Spree met the lake; some time alone to gather her thoughts might be enough before she returned to her mother. Whatever happened, she would apologise for the scene she'd caused on the beach. What had happened to Gerd wasn't her mother's fault, only hers.

She reached the water's edge. People all around her were smiling and happy. She wished more than anything she could feel the same way right now, desperate to take herself away from her troubles. A group of young men playfully jostled each other at the very end of the diving board. One pushed another into the water, then lost his balance in the act, following his friend into the lake. Those watching hooted with laughter.

Miriam suddenly felt warm and headed for a shaded part of the wall. She wondered what to do next. Small children hid from each other among the *Strandkörbe*. An old man woke with a start from his slumber and shooed them away, grumbling at the disturbance. Her feelings for Gerd were strong. At first, she'd had her doubts about the seemingly shifty side of his character, but the lengths to which he had ventured to ensure she'd been warned told her many things. She longed to see him again. If he really had been apprehended by the police because of what she'd said, he still cared enough to protect her. She had been told to be patient, that Gerd would come back, and that was enough for her.

If the security services knew what they were planning through Magda and her boyfriend's father, why hadn't Miriam been arrested? Her stomach sank. A small girl wandered past her, more ice cream around her face than in her mouth. She couldn't think about food. She felt everything was closing in on her and she had no idea what to do about it. In the end, she was certain about Gerd and she knew she wanted to leave. She let out a long sigh.

The time had come to level with her mother, even though Miriam was certain she wasn't going to like what she had to say.

***

He'd managed to track Walther down to his old stomping ground. He was holed up with an old buddy close to Kiefholzstrasse in

Kreuzberg. Gerd had a feeling Walther would be planning his next project and, whilst they were all together, he intended to confront them. The more he thought about it, the more he felt he needed to talk to Walther, to warn him. It hadn't entered Gerd's mind that anyone else in their immediate group could be an informer, but what Jack had said had made some sense, even though Gerd didn't want to believe it.

As she answered the door, a woman in her late fifties whipped off her apron, her greying blonde hair disappearing quickly under a headscarf. Gerd was about to say something but didn't get the chance.

'Another one for you, Walther. I'm going out!' she shouted behind her.

She ushered Gerd inside. 'Upstairs,' she nodded towards the back. Without giving him another glance, she grabbed a string shopping bag from the hook next to the door and was gone.

Gerd heard murmured voices and walked through the sparse, but spotlessly clean, kitchen to a staircase. As he headed upstairs, he could hear Walther's familiar tones taking the lead as usual.

Heidelberger Strasse wouldn't be an option for new tunnels for some time to come, if ever. The East German press had made their project into front-page news, and as much as Gerd hated to admit it, the *Fluchthelfer* community was licking its wounds after the spectacular "own goal" of their failed venture.

He reached the doorway of a small room. The talking stopped immediately as they recognised his presence. Walther was standing over the others; Arno, Peter and Jürgen were seated at a small table, looking at a diagram. There was another man Gerd didn't recognise.

Arno quickly flipped over the piece of paper, so it was blank side up. 'You've got some nerve showing up here,' he said with a snarl.

He knew what they would have been saying about him. Gerd knew how it worked and mud stuck fast. He had to face the problem head on.

He allowed his eyes to settle on Arno, before coolly turning to Walther. 'Could we talk?'

'We're busy here...'

Arno's words tailed off as Walther spoke. 'Gentlemen, if you wouldn't mind giving us five minutes.'

'You're not seriously going to give him the time of day?' Arno was incredulous.

Walther looked down at Arno and smiled. 'If you don't mind?'

Arno clearly did mind, but it was apparent that Walther was still in charge. The others shuffled back their chairs and made their way past Gerd at the door. Peter gave him a resigned smile, to which he nodded in reply. Perhaps not all of them believed what Arno was saying. Jürgen couldn't look him in the eye, however. Gerd tried to remain calm.

Arno was the last to leave, reluctant and suspicious, summoning a withering look for Gerd. In that small exchange, Gerd had seen something in Arno. He was melodramatic, almost like his outrage seemed feigned somehow, but there was something else. Gerd hadn't avoided eye contact as he had back at the pub; he stared right back at Arno and even allowed himself a half-smile. Gerd detected a flash of uncertainty, perhaps even fear in Arno's eyes.

With the others out of the room, Gerd pulled a chair up to the table.

'Already planning the next project?' Gerd said.

'You know Walther Noltke: he never stops.'

Gerd laughed. He felt calm, even though it was clear he'd been excluded from this gathering for a reason. 'You need to be more careful, Walther. It was close back there.'

'It wasn't the first time, and it won't be the last.'

The bravado was still there, but he detected something else in Walther. Gerd looked down at the piece of paper and wondered when the small talk would end. He decided to take the initiative.

'I would have thought I would have been the first name on your team sheet, Walther.'

He appeared uncomfortable now, even slightly ashamed. 'Look...'

'Don't explain, Walther. I already know what you're going to say.' Gerd sighed, summoning up energy from somewhere. 'I have to admit that cut me, Walther. I've known you and your family for a long time. I believe I never gave you any reason to doubt me during that time.'

'Never.'

'Yet here I am, excluded, after everything I've done to help this organisation. And all that for no personal gain.' Gerd gripped Walter's forearm now. 'I was helping people I didn't know, and probably never would, just like you, Walther.'

Walther's eyes were intense and wide, like a pair of serving plates. Gerd detected a colouring on his neck. 'I would have asked you, Gerd, you know that, but the others...'

Gerd shook his head. 'You're not weak like that, Walther. What you say goes.'

Perhaps the man was mortal after all. Even though Gerd felt resigned, he'd lost the deep anger and hurt of the previous day. It was a different emotion he felt now, and it surprised him somewhat. As Walther looked down to the floor, Gerd realised what it was. He felt pity for Walther Noltke, pity for his unending, somewhat fanatical, but flawed, need to push on despite the growing risks.

Gerd stood up. He'd planned to come here and put up an impassioned defence, to clear his name, but he had seen right from the off that it would be no use. Whatever he had said wouldn't have put him back on the team, but he didn't care anymore; for the first time he realised he didn't want to be part of it.

'I don't know what you think happened back there on Heidelberger Strasse, but I believe you know that whatever went wrong was nothing to do with me.'

Walther nodded slowly.

Gerd shook his head, recognising his friend's folly. 'If excluding me is the only change you've made since the last project then you haven't got rid of your leak.'

Walther looked up at him now, a flash of anger in his eyes. 'It could be anybody.'

'I agree. It's a shame Arno doesn't think like that.'

'He's just angry. He'll calm down. Maybe you can be back on the next dig...'

'No, Walther, I won't.' His voice was stern, and he was slightly surprised at his own strength of conviction. He jabbed his finger down on the table. 'I'm not one to cast unnecessary aspersions, because I know what that can do to a man's reputation...' Walther went to say something, but Gerd banged his fist down on the table, 'But if I were you, I'd have taken some time to check a few things before I rushed into something else.'

'What do you mean?'

'Why didn't we get a warning there were guards at the front of the shop, Walther? Who was on lookout?'

'Arno said he went to take a leak and by the time he'd seen them, it was too late.' He shrugged. 'It's a genuine excuse.'

'It's possible, Walther, yes. Like I said, I'm not one to make wild accusations.' Gerd paused. 'Unlike others.'

'You think it's Arno?'

Gerd shook his head. 'I'm not pointing the finger at anybody. It's up to you to sort that one out, not me.'

He walked towards the door.

'So, that's it?' Walther said.

'What do you mean, *"So, that's it"*? I'm the one who has been unjustly blamed for that fiasco, Walther. I didn't walk away, I was pushed.' He was at the door now. 'But you might want to consider something else about that night.'

Walther looked at him expectantly.

'Peter's sister was arrested, right?'

Walther was wary. 'Yes.'

'And also Jürgen's brother?'

'You know that.'

'What happened to Arno's family, Walther?'

***

She found her mother sitting with the others. She'd looked pleased to see Miriam, which was something at least. Some of the others looked embarrassed by her return; it was clear they'd been talking about the scene before. Her mother rose above all that and suggested they take a walk by the shore, just the two of them.

'I'd like that,' Miriam said.

There was a cool breeze, now, and that encouraged some to begin packing up for the day. The two of them walked close to the water's edge in silence for a while. It was hard to know where to start after their argument.

'I'm sorry for running off like that.'

Her mother nodded, seemingly accepting her apology, but Miriam could tell she was still shaken by what had happened.

'Also for what I said; it wasn't fair,' she added.

'No, it wasn't, but it's done now. Let's focus on putting things right.'

It was typical of her mother to be positive and constructive. Miriam did wonder if that would be her reaction after she'd told her everything. She felt bad, but it had to be said.

There were few swimmers now. The water had been a shock to the system in the middle of the day, let alone now the breeze had picked up. Miriam shivered, perhaps because of what she had to say to her mother.

Her mother linked her arm as they walked along the wet sand.

'So, are you going to tell me what's going on in that head of yours?'

Miriam sighed; it wasn't the time for half-measures. 'I'm in love with Gerd Braun.'

Her mother stopped walking. 'You've still being seeing him?'

'Please, Mum, don't be mad at me. This is already hard enough.'

Her mother's face was serious and taut, but she nodded and continued their walk, albeit more slowly; perhaps it was trepidation.

'The reason I've been upset is because I was going to escape… to the West.'

'What? Are you mad?'

'Just listen to me, will you?' Miriam pleaded. 'You might not like what I have to say, but I need to tell you.'

Her mother's eyes rolled, and Miriam knew she was itching to interrupt, but she held back.

'I was supposed to leave this weekend…'

'Leave how?' Her mother's voice cracked. 'Why couldn't you tell me?'

'I wanted to, but I only thought you'd stop me, tell me the same old things about how life would be good for me here, but it won't, Mum. There's nothing here anymore.'

An older couple were folding up blankets and the woman looked over towards them. Her mother led Miriam further away from twitching ears.

'Do you know how dangerous this is, what you're saying?'

Miriam was nodding. 'That's part of the problem.'

'I can't believe it's got this bad.' Her mother put her hand to her forehead.

'Well, you have had other things on your mind.'

'No, Miriam, that's not fair,' her mother snapped.

Miriam looked out over the water and sighed. 'Look, I didn't come back here to argue with you.'

'And I don't want to argue with you, but you've got to know what you're saying, what you're planning, is illegal. They could arrest you!'

Miriam looked down towards her feet. 'Magda knows.'

Her mother closed her eyes and sighed. When she started she was quiet and seemingly struggling to contain her anger. 'These are not just teenage games, Miriam. This is very real and very dangerous.'

Miriam went to speak then closed her mouth. She couldn't begin to explain what she thought had happened to Gerd or about the man in the hardware shop. This wasn't the time or the place.

'Miriam, you really need to think about what you're doing here…'

'I know exactly what I'm doing. I want to leave.' She surprised herself with her resolve.

She even dared to look at her mother. The hair was over her face and there were tears forming in her eyes. Now Miriam felt terrible, even though she wasn't about to change her mind. She went to hug her mother, but she pushed her away.

'I am having difficulty believing what I'm hearing right now.'

'I know. It must be hard.' Miriam's voice was subdued.

Tears rolled openly down her mother's cheeks. It was the first time Miriam could ever remember having seen her cry.

'I can't believe you want to leave me,' she sobbed.

CHAPTER 27

JUNE 1962, WEST BERLIN

Gerd Braun found himself sitting in a stand at the back of the Olympiastadion, watching a parade of British soldiers on the Maifeld. Soldiers marched in perfect lines, wearing black fur hats and thick red coats with white belts. To top it off, some of them were wearing a heavy, woollen skirt. Gerd couldn't help wondering what all the pomp and ceremony was about. He knew why he was here, at least, and that was because Ulrich Schultz had invited him.

Ulrich leant close to him with his hand over his mouth. 'It's the birthday of the British queen.'

Gerd couldn't help raising his eyebrows. 'They do this every year?'

'Their queen is very important to the British.'

'She must be, for the men to wear a skirt,' Gerd said in all innocence.

Ulrich laughed. 'It's called a kilt.'

Gerd shook his head. It all seemed a long way from his world.

The meeting with Walther had strengthened his resolve. Gerd still respected Walther and what he was trying to achieve, but felt he was better off out of their next project. Perhaps it was the fact Walther didn't have an answer for his reasoned response and questions about Arno. Walther had shown himself to be slightly flawed in his approach. At least Gerd was back where he felt comfortable – operating independently, looking out for his own back. He would get Miriam out and he swore he would be the one to effect her escape.

At a break in proceedings, Ulrich led him away from the Maifeld towards the stadium proper, so they could talk. Gerd filled Ulrich in on the Heidelberger Strasse fiasco and what had happened at the subsequent meeting with Walther.

Ulrich seemed engrossed but didn't comment.

'I've got a lot of time for Walther, and some of the others are decent blokes but…' Gerd didn't feel the need to finish the sentence. 'Anyway, that's all in the past. I need you to find me another tunnel project.' He turned to Ulrich. 'I need to get Miriam out of there.'

Ulrich grimaced. 'Well, that's not going to be easy.'

'You must know of other projects I could join.'

'Perhaps,' said Ulrich, without committing himself either way. 'But as you know from personal experience, these groups are tight, not exactly open to outsiders.'

Away to their right, work was going on to rebuild the Olympic tower. British engineers had blown it up after the war due to its links with the Nazis. Gerd did wonder why they felt now was the right time to reconstruct it.

'I have another favour to ask,' Gerd said cautiously, worried how the request might be received.

'Well?'

'I'd like to see Miriam.'

Once again, Ulrich didn't commit either way. 'Understandable, I suppose.'

'You think it's possible?'

'Why not?'

Gerd still wasn't sure what to think of Ulrich. He wondered if all spies were like this.

'You know you'll have to see Weber again?'

He was resigned for that unfortunate downside to seeing Miriam, but if it meant he could see her once more, to reassure her, to hold her, he was prepared to do it.

Ulrich stopped. 'You'll have to go with something to offer. It's what he's waiting for.'

'I won't tell him anything about Walther and what they're planning at Kiefholzstrasse. Anyway, I don't know the detail.'

'It's better that way. No suspicion will fall on you when it goes wrong.'

Gerd hadn't thought about it that way. 'You think it will? Go wrong, I mean?'

Ulrich shrugged. 'From what you've told me, they haven't dealt with the problem.'

Gerd didn't feel at all good about that, but he'd warned Walther; he could do no more for him.

'So, how do we go about this?' Gerd asked.

'There's no easy way. We have a lot of work to do before you step foot back in East Berlin.'

Gerd was started to feel concerned, and it must have shown on his face.

Ulrich laughed. 'Don't worry, Gerd. I will push you hard, but I've got just the thing for Weber.'

***

There was a keen wind on the observation deck of the Funkturm. It was likely to be the case over one hundred metres up. It had been a while since he'd looked out over Berlin. In the western part of the city, building continued apace, the *Wirtschaftswunder*, the economic miracle, still applied. Jack could see over towards the Olympiastadion, wondering how much this part of the world had suffered since Jesse Owens went back home with a bag full of medals.

'You choose your places, Jack.' His brother-in-law looked wary, if slightly intrigued.

'I thought you might appreciate some privacy,' Jack said.

'Why would there be need for privacy for a family get-together?' Ulrich said with feigned innocence. 'Or do you have an ulterior motive?'

Gerd had returned from his meeting with Walther seemingly steeled by what had happened. The look and manner of the old Gerd had returned, perhaps without the cheeky smiles. Jack was feeling his way to a good solution for his friend, Miriam Hirsch, and if it really worked, also Hans Erdmann.

Jack tutted. 'That's the trouble with your fraternity, always suspicious.'

Ulrich laughed. 'I suppose it beats the cynicism of journalism.'

'Ouch!'

'How are Eva and the little one?'

'They're good, but you should come and see for yourself seeing as you're in Berlin.' Jack was enjoying playing games with Ulrich.

It drew a look. 'I don't usually advertise the fact, for obvious reasons.'

Jack pushed a coin into the standing binoculars and peered over towards the East, past the Brandenburg Gate. Great swathes of the city still sat empty, devoid of life except for overgrowing vegetation.

'So, why the invitation?'

'To the point as always, Ulrich. You young ones are too impatient these days.'

'I'm not that much younger than you. Perhaps I'm just more wily than in my youth, maybe it's the job, maybe it's the invitation to meet my brother-in-law at the top of the Funkturm.'

Jack turned towards him, took Ulrich by the shoulders, and said dramatically. 'That's because I have a proposal for you, dear Ulrich.'

Ulrich rolled his eyes. 'I can't imagine my boss will like the sound of this.'

'So don't tell him.'

'What scheme have you got cooking this time?'

Jack had one last look around him. They were alone on the platform except for an excited kid with his mother, who didn't sound too keen to spend a second longer up there. 'I've been racking my brains trying to think who has good connections with the *Fluchthelfer* community. Someone who is likely to know what's going on in Berlin, under Berlin, if you know what I'm saying.'

Ulrich was already shaking his head. 'You know I can't talk about my work, Jack.'

Jack held up his hands. 'I'm not asking you to talk about it. You just need to listen to me.'

Ulrich appeared reluctant to even do that.

'Come on, what have you got to lose?'

'My job... my sanity.'

'Apart from that?' Jack laughed. 'It's good you've not lost your humour.'

'I suspect I'm going to need it.'

'By the time this afternoon is done, you're going to be thanking me. Believe me,' Jack said.

***

They were lower down the tower now in the bustling cafeteria. Jack had paid for lunch for the two of them, but Ulrich remained cagey, as always.

'So, let me get this straight: you're asking for help to get as yet unknown parties over?' There was no mention of walls or escaping here, just in case.

Jack corrected him. 'Not help from your people directly.'

'From contacts I might have that are mid-project, let's say.'

Jack nodded, dropping a sugar cube into his coffee.

Ulrich was shaking his head again. Jack noticed he did that a lot. Maybe it was Jack's influence on him.

'You know what these people are like, Jack. They're obsessive about security. I doubt they would let any outsiders near their project.'

'I just need an introduction.'

Ulrich sighed. 'They're going to want to know who the people are.'

'For the right price, I am sure they could be persuaded.'

'I want to know who the people are.' Ulrich's voice was stern.

Jack smiled then leant towards him and whispered, 'Gerd Braun's girlfriend.'

Ulrich's eyes narrowed. Jack knew he was wondering if Gerd had told him about Ulrich's involvement.

'Come on, Uli, when Klaus went to see Markus, it wasn't that difficult to work out it was you whom Gerd would meet.'

Ulrich didn't say a word, his face impassive.

'I don't want you to tell me anything, and to be clear, Gerd himself has said nothing about you.'

Ulrich moved, but only to pick up his coffee cup. It was like playing poker.

'You said "people",' Ulrich finally murmured. 'Who else?'

'Hans Erdmann,' Jack said out of the side of his mouth.

Ulrich was shaking his head again. 'Jack, you've got to be kidding. You know he has links with Burzin. He's KGB, for God's sake. Why would anybody stick their neck out for him?'

Jack shrugged. 'Maybe you should ask your father.'

'How's Dad involved?'

'He's not, if I can help it.'

Ulrich smiled briefly, recognising the likely conflict behind Jack's words.

'Your father feels he owes Erdmann. He was a big part in the reason Eva made it out, Ulrich. Hell, I believe I owe the man something.'

Jack pressed on, 'It could mean a promotion, Ulrich. Imagine, helping an NVA colonel to defect. Think about the intelligence he would bring.'

Ulrich scoffed. 'If Burzin tried to help him get out last time, there was a reason for that.'

That was not something Jack had considered.

'All right, let's put that to one side for the moment. Let's talk about the people involved in these projects. Do you have somebody in mind who could help us?'

'Help *you*, Jack. Let's be clear, if – and it's a very big if at the moment – I introduce you, it's just that. The rest of it you can deal with yourself.'

'That's okay for me, but I think you're forgetting the fact that Gerd needs help. He's my friend, but he saved my wife, your sister's, life that night.'

Ulrich shifted uncomfortably in his seat. Jack knew he had hit a sore spot.

'He's in trouble and we have to do what we can for him.'

Ulrich looked around him and Jack did wonder if he'd finally broken through his brother-in-law's professional armour.

'This doesn't sit right with me, Jack. I feel uneasy. As much as I admire your ideals, and sometimes your instinct, your profession is slightly off-putting.'

Ulrich's face was serious, and Jack couldn't help laughing. 'I admit they don't exactly go hand in hand, but I'm not operating in a professional capacity on this one, and forgive me if I'm wrong, but I suspect whatever you are doing for Gerd, you're doing it on a personal, not professional, level.'

Ulrich shot him a warning look.

'Come on, Uli, the kid's not even seventeen! There's no way the BND would sanction any operation. They would tell you to steer well clear.'

Ulrich looked away. He was wavering, and Jack knew it.

'So, do you want to hear the rest, or not?'

'Do I have a choice?'

'Not really,' Jack said with a beaming smile. 'Now, of the projects ongoing at the moment, I would guess you're permitted to provide some assistance, help them along with certain things, but unofficially.'

Ulrich nodded warily. 'It's how we get to know what's going on. Anyway, we have to vet the refugees who do make it through.'

Jack was nodding. 'As I thought. What you cannot do, I would guess, is provide funds for these ventures. Some of which, the better engineered ones, will be costly.'

'That would be a fair assumption.'

Jack felt satisfied with himself. 'So, there we have it.'

'Are you telling me you're going to provide funds for a project?' Ulrich said doubtfully.

'Not me, but I know a man who can.'

'With certain conditions…'

'A place on the team for Gerd, and safe passage for the people I mentioned.'

Ulrich sighed. 'I know these guys; they'd shoot their own mother if they thought they'd be betrayed. They won't take kindly to conditions.'

Jack winked. 'Money talks, Ulrich.'

CHAPTER 28

JULY 1962, EAST BERLIN

Gerd wondered if he'd made the right decision. Ulrich had prepared him tirelessly, talking through every eventuality. Despite that, it was still with a sense of foreboding that he approached the checkpoint on Sonnenallee. It was all pre-arranged of course; Weber had given him precise instructions of what to do when he was ready to return to East Berlin. This was a quieter checkpoint, one away from the prying eyes of Heinrich Heine Strasse or Friedrichstrasse. In the end, this was the only way he could see Miriam in the short term.

After making Gerd wait, sweating in a side room at the checkpoint, Weber duly arrived. He was dressed in a light suit, sweat patches showing at the front of his shirt. There was no doubting his authority in these circles; the guards moved fast to implement his orders, and Gerd was sitting in Weber's light grey Wartburg in no time at all.

'You took your time, young Braun,' Weber said sternly.

'Good information takes time to gather,' Gerd said, staring out at the streets on which he once spent so much time.

'I hope you have something worthwhile.'

'I came back to see Miriam,' Gerd said with confidence.

Weber scoffed. 'That's not how it works; information first, then, and only then, might we let you see the Hirsch girl, with supervision, of course.'

'Stop the car!' Gerd shouted.

Weber flashed him a look as if he were mad.

'I said, pull over!'

Weber did as Gerd said, seemingly as much in shock as anything else.

'Now, I have something for you, but this is how it will work…'

Weber was shaking his head. 'You're not in control of this situation…'

'A tunnel,' Gerd said quickly.

Weber went quiet, sweat beads on his forehead. He finally whispered, 'Noltke?' like an aged archaeologist talking about the Holy Grail.

'Not this time, but nonetheless a Girmann operation.'

Weber's eyes widened at the name.

'It makes no sense for us to be seen together. I'm going to get out of the car and find my own way to Miriam. It might take some time; after all, I don't know exactly where she is. When I find her, it is your responsibility to ensure we are not harassed by any of your men.'

Weber shifted in his seat, the springs squawking in protest.

'When I get back, I assume to Sonnenallee?'

Weber nodded eagerly.

'When I get back, I will give you all the details of where you can find the tunnel.'

Weber took a deep breath, then turned to Gerd and growled, 'We're watching her. Remember we can bring her in at any time.'

Gerd stymied his anger. 'I know the situation. I know where I stand. You have to understand it makes sense to do it like this for all concerned.'

Weber licked his lips nervously, still thinking things over. Gerd's heart was beating fast. The whole plan relied on Weber buying this.

Weber finally nodded his assent.

It had gone just like Ulrich said it would. Gerd went to get out of the car, not without a sense of relief.

Suddenly, Weber's hand shot out and he gripped Gerd's forearm tightly. 'I'm trusting you, Braun,' he growled. 'Don't let me down, or the ending will not be nice for you, or Miriam.'

***

Hans Erdmann had envisaged a romantic dinner for two, an evening where he could get closer to Hannah Hirsch. Since that day at the beach, Hannah's demeanour had changed markedly. Hans sensed it could only have been related to her daughter, Miriam. Immediately after their long talk on the shores of the Mügelsee, she had seemed deflated and somewhat distracted. Yet, somewhere in his mistrustful mind he still wondered if this was all real.

She was still open to having dinner, but Hannah suggested they meet at her apartment because in her words, she "didn't feel like going out". It confirmed to him that her low mood was more likely to do with Miriam than anything he'd done. He couldn't help being intrigued by what had happened between mother and daughter. It was clear that changing the demeanour of somebody as resolute as Hannah Hirsch would take something serious.

The apartment building looked down onto the tramlines of Bahnhofstrasse in Pankow. It was a four-storey affair and had managed to survive the war well, aside from the odd score from a stray bullet. It was a higher standard of living quarters than most were used to in East Berlin and reinforced the connections Hannah must have; apartments in this condition were not available to the ordinary person. As he pressed the buzzer, he did wonder what the atmosphere might be like if Miriam was there.

Hannah greeted him at the door with a quick peck on the cheek and then a prolonged hug.

'Come in,' she said. 'Dinner is just about ready. It will be simple I'm afraid; I'm not known for my skills in the kitchen.'

Hans could smell fried potatoes and his mouth watered. He suspected more effort had gone into the meal than Hannah had cared to reveal; potatoes were not readily available.

'I'm finishing in here,' she called from the small kitchen area.

Hans stood in the doorway and she handed him a beer with a slightly sad smile.

'Miriam not around?'

'She went out earlier. I didn't want her to go but…' Her words trailed off as she pushed a sausage around the pan, her shoulders slumped. He wondered what type of night it was going to be with Hannah in this mood.

In the end, Hans enjoyed the potato rösti and sausage with mustard. It was a rare treat. Hannah didn't manage to eat so much, her mind clearly elsewhere. After clearing away the dishes together, the two of them returned to the table. Hannah reached out for his hand, and he was convinced she was going to cry.

'I've held this in for two days since Miriam told me. I wasn't sure who I could tell…' Hannah looked up. '…or even trust with it.'

Hans took a long swig from a bottle of beer, transfixed. She had his attention. He felt like he probably should have murmured that he could be trusted, but something like that, especially in East Berlin, could only be decided by the person telling their story. Words alone meant little.

'There's no two ways to say this. Miriam has told me she wants to leave.'

'Leave? To go where?'

Hannah gave him a stern look and the penny slowly rolled down a shallow decline in his brain and finally dropped.

'I mean what you said at the beach and I told you not to be ridiculous.'

She gripped his hand tighter.

'Oh,' was all Hans could manage.

'Hans, what am I going to do?' The tears pricked in the corner of her eyes and spilt out over her cheeks. Hans moved his chair away from the table and instinctively Hannah fell towards him, squeezing him with the strength of a bear. He embraced her, feeling her predicament, but he couldn't prevent his mind exploring the possibilities her revelation opened up. He knew it wasn't right, but he couldn't help himself.

'How exactly does she intend to do it?' Hans asked cautiously.

Hannah was still sobbing slightly, but had regained her composure. 'The boy I told you about will help her.'

Hans wondered just how to handle this. He couldn't quite believe it was real. 'It's a dangerous game, Hannah.'

'That's exactly what I told her, but her heart appears set on it.'

'Does she realise what she's got herself into?'

She looked at him now, her eyes almost pleading for some kind of forgiveness. 'I even thought of going to the police, Hans. Can you imagine that? Your own flesh and blood.'

Having this conversation was illegal in the DDR. By discussing the subject with him, on the one hand, she had implicated him if he didn't report it, whereas on the other, she had shown a trust in him. It was the type of conversation that tied the fates of individuals. He watched her every move. It felt genuine. After all, how could she pull her daughter into all this so convincingly if she was working for the Stasi?

'As much as I can understand that you're hurting, I don't think that would be a good idea.'

Hannah didn't really register his advice; perhaps she expected that response. Her emotions were probably too raw to think rationally. Hans could do nothing to prevent the surge of excitement inside him. Could this be possible?

'How could she, Hans? How could she just leave me? I would… never see her again. Am I being selfish here?'

The question was ironic, given that Hans himself had tried to escape East Berlin less than a year before.

'I can understand how you feel…'

'I don't care about what the authorities would do about my job. It's not important. I just thought Miriam and I were close.'

Hannah looked like a shell of her former self. Hans wondered just how she'd managed to function over the last couple of days. Now, however, his mind was racing on. He wanted to ask many questions. Exactly how Miriam planned to escape. Why had Miriam decided to tell her, and why then? Had she told anybody else? It had crossed his mind that she might have a Stasi tail. He breathed deeply. As much as he wanted to press her, it wasn't the right time.

'Come on,' he said, pulling her close. 'You did the right thing in telling me. We'll get it sorted out. It's going to be okay, Hannah.'

She sighed. It was what she needed to hear. Hans meant it, but maybe his idea of a good solution wasn't one Hannah could envisage. Not yet, anyway.

***

After assuring her mother she wasn't about to do anything stupid, Miriam had set off walking. Since she'd told her mother, she felt terrible. She hadn't quite expected this reaction. Now she felt like a selfish little girl bringing unnecessary heartache to her family. It had never been her intention to cause hurt, yet her mother's reaction hadn't changed her mind. She'd felt a profound sense of relief after telling her, and now she'd made her decision, Miriam felt stronger, convinced she was doing the right thing.

Hans Erdmann was coming for dinner and she hoped that would cheer her mother up somewhat. She knew she couldn't possibly tell him the truth of what had gone on between them; that would be suicide for all concerned.

Miriam had taken the S-Bahn into the city. She wandered through Alexanderplatz, doing her very best to ignore the plethora of propaganda posters. They proclaimed "Socialism is working"; maybe for some, but not for her. She looked longingly across to the spot in front of the HO store where her and Gerd had last hugged. She couldn't help wondering when she'd be able to get away from this place.

It hadn't been a conscious decision, but she found herself ambling to all the spots her and Gerd had spent time together, where they'd talked and laughed together, where they'd shared their hopes and dreams for the future. Now they were just memories, albeit very agreeable ones.

It was a pleasant evening and she was content to lose herself for a time. She didn't trust herself enough to venture anywhere near the border in case she had a mad rush of blood and decided to scale the wall. She saw the tram appear, slowing to a halt in front of the Rotes Rathaus. On a whim, she ran to catch up with the last passengers getting on. As the tram pulled away, she smiled to herself. She would go to the place where her and Gerd had first kissed. Her stomach flipped at the thought.

CHAPTER 29

JUNE 1962, WEST BERLIN

It was getting late. With Eva on a night shift, Jack had long since put Tanja to bed. He was doing his best to busy himself working at the table. It was a forlorn attempt. He was actually trying to avoid Klaus, but that wasn't easy in the confines of the apartment. He felt they had said all they had to say to each other, especially on the topic of Hans Erdmann.

Jack looked up from the typewriter to see Klaus leave the bathroom and place his bag by the door. Jack's spirits surged; he couldn't help it. He immediately felt guilty and admonished himself mildly for being too harsh.

'Going somewhere, Klaus?' It felt like a loaded question, such was the atmosphere.

'Early flight back,' he explained.

He suddenly felt bad for all the grumbling he'd done about Klaus over the past week. He knew Tanja for one would be heartbroken when her grandfather left.

Klaus hesitated, then crossed the carpet of the lounge to join him at the table.

Jack sensed a moment between them. 'Drink?'

Klaus nodded.

Jack fetched the rare bottle of VAT 69 from the sideboard and poured each of them a generous measure. He wasn't sure if it might be interpreted as a celebration. They drank in silence for a while, each seemingly waiting for the other to talk. It didn't help that Klaus was a man of few words. That's why he was surprised when Klaus started. 'I've been hard on you, Jack.'

Jack nearly dropped his glass. He couldn't think of a reasoned response, such was his shock.

'I'm not just talking about now, but from the beginning.' He went to say something, but Klaus just shook his head. 'Not that I'm apologising for it.' He shrugged. 'It's the way I am now.'

Jack felt some relief; normality reigned finally. He had wondered if Klaus had been transforming himself in the bathroom.

'This thing about Erdmann, it's difficult to explain.'

Jack swilled his whisky around the glass. 'Why don't you try?'

Klaus thought about it then picked up his glass and downed the contents. Without asking, he picked up the bottle and poured himself a copious measure, larger than the first. Jack winced at the profligacy and hoped it would be worth it.

'We left so many men behind in Russia, most of them after Stalingrad. You know one of my comrades drowned in a camp latrine?'

The thought made Jack feel sick. The details of misery were never pleasant.

'Anyway, my point is, Erdmann is one of us. He might be over there, KGB, or whatever, but deep down he suffered in the camps, like Markus and me. I'd have been back home in a couple of years, like Erdmann, if it hadn't been for Dobrovsky.'

'If they had let you go with the others, would you have stayed in a socialist Germany?' Jack was genuinely intrigued.

It brought a hard stare. 'Not a chance.'

In this candid moment between them, Jack wondered if this was the time to share the news of the progress he'd made, but he was reluctant. Even though Ulrich had received the green light from the tunnellers to talk, he'd been trying to track down Harry O'Donnell for the past few days, without success.

'If there's anybody that would understand about Erdmann, it's me, Klaus. I left comrades behind in Korea, too.'

He nodded, without seemingly registering the point. Apparently, there was something he had to get out. 'If I can do something to help an old comrade I will go out of my way, and that's why I've been a bit... pushy.'

Jack could think of stronger words to describe his father-in-law's behaviour, but now didn't feel like the right time to voice them.

'So, why are you heading home now?'

Klaus shrugged. 'I've got work to do for one.' He was quiet for a moment, then he peered at Jack over the rim of his glass. 'Maybe I trust you to sort it out on your own, without me in the way.'

It was only a "maybe", but Jack had a job to prevent himself choking on the whisky. This was as close to a compliment as it got. In fact, he may as well have pinned an Iron Cross to Jack's front.

Jack was still in shock and maybe that's why he thought it was the right time to update Klaus. After all, when the time came, he would need Klaus if they were to contact Erdmann.

'I'm close to something, Klaus.'

He raised his eyebrows. 'That's good.'

'For Gerd and Hans.'

Klaus nodded. 'Well, if you need me, you know where I am.'

For a week, Jack had been hoping to hear those words; now it felt different. 'When it's arranged, I'll need you to contact Burzin.' He shrugged. 'I assume it's the only way to Erdmann.'

Klaus sighed. 'I suppose so, though that old bugger Burzin has such a sharp sense of timing, he'll probably call me first.'

Jack laughed, feeling kinship with his father-in-law. Maybe the two of them were too alike and that's why they clashed, although Jack shuddered to think he was anything like his father-in-law.

The phone rang, and he almost felt sad their moment had been interrupted.

'Kaymer,' he answered with a sigh.

'Jack, it's Jimmy down at the Eden.' A saxophone was blasting its solo in the background.

'Jimmy, what can I do for you?' He was still mildly irritated at the late-night interruption, and it was apparent in his voice.

'It's the other way round, mate.' The young English student had been employed to keep the international clientele content. Jack struggled to catch his accent sometimes.

'What?'

'Never mind.' There was an interlude of ragged applause and shrill whistling which pierced Jack's ear.

'I can hardly hear you, Jimmy.'

'That TV guy you were asking about yesterday.'

'What about him?'

'He's at the bar. Although I'd get down here sharpish if I were you. He's had a few already.'

The line went dead.

***

For once, Jack had been grateful for Klaus's presence. It was with a slightly heavy heart he left his father-in-law in charge of his daughter and his best whisky. He headed for Wilmersdorf. The Eden, or the Old Eden as it was now known, had recently moved from Nestorstrasse to Damaschkestrasse, on the other side of the Ku'damm. It wasn't far, but Rolf Eden needed to make way for his ever-growing chain of bars. It was a place Jack tended to shy away from – there were too many spooks, journalists and general big shots who liked to frequent the place for his liking – but now he'd finally tracked Harry O'Donnell down, he had little choice in the matter.

He managed to park up close to the bar, so much so he could see the neon Englehardt Brewery sign on the bar's frontage. As he approached, a young couple smooched against the railings. There was giggling, then a sharp word of admonishment from the woman; seemingly the man's hand had wandered where it shouldn't have. Jack headed on down the stairs.

After the relative peace of the street, the cacophony of the live band and the clientele shouting to make themselves heard was like a slap in the face. The Eden was packed to the rafters. Jack looked to the bar only to see Jimmy, the man who'd called him, with his hands full keeping up with service. He scanned his eyes around the place. The three-piece band were seated, playing on a raised stage, their heads squeezed in below the graffiti-covered ceiling. A Charlie Chaplin film was projected on a screen near to the band. Lampshades, some with photographs stuck to them, hung at different heights. Amongst the throng, it was proving difficult to locate the elusive Harry. Jack hoped he hadn't already left.

He nudged his way through the revellers. A young woman sat at the bar, drinking beer from a large, dimpled glass, leaning on the shoulder of a journalist Jack knew. His wife wasn't there, which wasn't exactly a surprise; the Eden wasn't a place men took their wives. Smoke hung above the bar in a constant haze. He was still trying to attract Jimmy's attention, but there were at least five others doing that, trying to get a drink.

Then there was no need for Jimmy's help. Even above the din, he heard raised voices in the corner. Harry O'Donnell was swaying on a high stool, a rather full glass hanging precariously in his hand. A tall man stood close to him looking rather aggrieved. Jack had a feeling it may have been to do with the wet patch down the front of his nicely pressed trousers, and that ultimately Harry had been involved somewhere down the line. The man was over six feet and looking increasingly aggressive; his head was at the side of a black and yellow lightshade with "Sputnik" daubed across it. For the moment, a lady was trying to calm the man down. Harry O'Donnell was oblivious.

Jack heard shrieks of shock and the clatter of glass before he could reach the corner. He had a bad feeling. The crowd of people standing close to the tall tables had parted. Jack reached the edge of the circle to see Harry sprawling on the floor, giggling like a naughty school boy.

'Reet, that's et!' The big man dragged Harry to his feet. Jack's heart sank. The man's accent was Scottish, probably part of the British forces in the city. His blonde hair was tinged with red and Jack swore he saw steam coming from the man's nose. He held the wriggling Harry by the scruff of his collar. Nobody appeared willing to intervene this time.

With great reluctance, Jack stepped forward. 'Okay, buddy, let me take him out of your way.'

The affronted man turned to Jack and snarled, 'Not before I've dropped the bastard!'

'Heh, I said leave him to me!' Jack snapped, trying to sound tough, but only fearing the worst.

The man's grip on Harry loosened slightly. 'Stay oot of this, Yank!'

Out of the corner of his eye, Jack had spotted two of the club's doormen making their way over. One of them nodded to Jack. They stood behind him, facing the man, their arms crossed.

The Scottish man thought about it for a moment, then shoved Harry roughly towards Jack. 'He's a lucky wee boy, and so are yee,' he growled.

***

It had taken two hours and three rounds of strong coffee to get Harry O'Donnell anywhere near coherent. Jack was growing tired of it, but knew the man held the key to his plan. The late-night café was nearly empty.

'We could have stayed at the Eden,' Harry slurred forlornly.

'Not without you getting killed, we couldn't.'

Harry laughed. 'Ah, he was just a pussycat.'

'You might see it differently in the morning.'

He screwed up his face as he tasted the coffee. 'Don't they have any whisky in this place?'

'You've had enough, Harry.'

'Says who?' he growled. 'Anyway, what do you want, Jack? I was happy back there.'

'You don't look that happy to me.'

Harry's face softened. 'That bitch is playing up with the kids. She wants more money before she lets me see them.'

'Yeah, well maybe I can help you there,' Jack said, itching to get to the point.

Harry grimaced. 'I doubt it. Ricksen called me yesterday complaining about the lack of a big story. He's called me home, Jack.'

'He's fired you?'

'As much as. I fly home next week.'

Jack reached over the table and shook him. 'Well, you're going to have to damned well convince him otherwise.'

'And how am I going to do that?'

'I've got a meeting tomorrow morning.'

Harry looked at him quizzically, still evidently gripped in the confused haze of alcohol.

'I think I've found you a tunnel, Harry.'

CHAPTER 30

JULY 1962, EAST BERLIN

Gerd couldn't believe it had gone so smoothly. Weber had accepted his approach, as Ulrich had predicted he would, and aside from the obligatory threats, he had allowed him to pass on into East Berlin alone. It was not that Gerd trusted Weber in the slightest, but whatever he said, he had to appear genuine; he knew, and Weber kindly reminded him at every opportunity, that Miriam's future liberty was at stake. If the plan was to work in the end, she had to be free. Gerd just hoped that Ulrich had given him real information to feed to Weber, and that would placate the Stasi man. He knew he was in a precarious place.

It was a strange position to be in, able to roam the streets of East Berlin with the blessing of the Stasi. Now Gerd had to tackle the difficult part; find Miriam, which would be hard enough. Then, probably, he had to lose her tail; he didn't believe for a second, in spite of his agreement to the contrary, that Weber would call off the agents watching her. This would be a test of all that Ulrich had taught him in the short window of time that had been available to them.

At Miriam's Pankow apartment, it didn't take long to establish the surveillance on her was still operational. Fortunately, the man in question was quite obvious about it; dressed in a suit and coat more suitable for March, he was reading a paper, leaning against the S-Bahn stop. He didn't get on when the tram arrived, either. It told Gerd Miriam was more than likely to be at home. It was just a question of sitting things out now.

He could feel the excitement in his stomach at the mere chance of seeing her again. So much had happened since they'd last been together; it had barely been two weeks, yet it felt like a lifetime. No matter how hard he tried, the doubts remained. Despite his best efforts, he still had no idea if Miriam intended to leave for the West. He knew even if she did leave the apartment it would be difficult to talk alone for any length of time. The real aim of the visit was not about satisfying Gerd's wish to see her, but to clarify her intentions.

It was late afternoon when the Stasi man was relieved by his colleague. Even from a distance, Gerd could see the men acknowledge each other. The new man was much shorter, but still sported the same cheap suit and overcoat. Watching their behaviour, he wondered if Weber had purposely ignored his plea to call his men off or if the message just hadn't got through. From what he'd witnessed, with their openness and lack of the tradecraft Ulrich had spoken about so much, he was beginning to suspect the Stasi weren't as efficient as people thought.

Gerd realised he'd not eaten since morning, but the tension was keeping him going. Unlike Miriam's Stasi watchers, he'd changed his position a number of times. He was attempting to stay out of view whilst maintaining his watch on the apartment.

It was half an hour later when she finally appeared. Gerd did his best to stifle his feelings of pure relief at seeing her, noting she looked so well. She had a jacket over her shoulder and headed towards the S-Bahn stop. He wanted to give her a warning about her tail, but now wasn't the time. As much as he wanted to run over there and embrace her, it would have to wait for a more opportune moment, if it ever presented itself.

Miriam looked as bright as ever. Gerd smiled to himself, knowing all the lengths to which he'd gone to be there were worth it and more. As the tram approached, Gerd left his cover, pulling up his collar. Miriam and her Stasi tail took the first carriage, Gerd slipping onto the second at the final moment. He took a seat close to the front next to an old lady, the best place to keep tabs on the two of them up ahead.

The tram headed for the centre of town through Prenzlauer Berg. Gerd felt he might only have one chance to speak to Miriam. He just had to be close enough to take it. He felt calm and in control. He had no reason to fear being found in East Berlin; this was more about doing things under the noses of the Stasi. It gave him a thrill as he thought about it.

Close to Alexanderplatz, Miriam got up. Most other passengers were also preparing to alight which helped Gerd maintain his own cover. He stepped off the tram, helping the old lady down, who smiled a toothless, sincere smile. Miriam was heading at a leisurely place towards the Berolinahaus, her tail ten metres behind her. Gerd hung back, close to the tram stop, then crossed the traffic towards the HO department store. Now he felt more anxious about how he might achieve what he came to do.

He could see her walking under the railway bridge, the station above. She stopped and looked over towards his position. Quickly he slipped behind a propaganda hoarding, for once thankful for their abundance. He wondered if she'd seen him for a brief moment. He could see her gazing thoughtfully, then he realised she was looking over towards the department store entrance. It was the last place they'd been together; if only she knew just how close he was now.

She set off again, ambling almost, as if she wasn't heading to any place in particular. It made her easy to follow. Gerd cast his eyes back to Miriam's tail. He seemed nonchalant. Probably he'd been following this teenage girl around for the last fortnight. Maybe he felt there was no apparent reason. It wouldn't make it any easier for Gerd to get to her.

After passing under the bridge on the opposite side of the street, Gerd could see Miriam was heading in the direction of the Marienkirche. He rushed to get closer. She was heading for the doorway at the front of the red-bricked building. He crossed over Karl-Liebknecht-Strasse, keeping his distance. She sat down on a low wall close to the entrance; the Stasi man continued on past. He sat down some metres away and took out his newspaper. Gerd wondered if this might be his chance. If he could find a way of obscuring himself against the wall of church, visible to Miriam but not to her tail, it might just work.

He reached the side of the church, now out of sight of Miriam. He had to be careful now. When he made it the front edge of the church he would be very close to her. He couldn't startle her, as that might, in turn, alert the Stasi man to his presence. He moved as quickly as he could down the edge of the church, under its dark stained-glass windows. When he reached the corner of the building, he held his breath for a moment, then he popped his head around edge of the brickwork. Miriam had gone.

Gerd quickly scanned across to where the Stasi man was seated. He was already up and discarding his newspaper in haste. He started to run over the square on the other side of the church. Where was Miriam? Gerd slid around the front, desperate to see where she'd gone.

The Stasi man was running away from him towards the Rotes Rathaus. It was then he spotted Miriam on the other side of the trees heading for a tram; the last passengers were getting on. The Stasi man was some twenty metres behind her.

Miriam just made it to the tram before it set off. Her pursuer had only managed to reach the opposite side of the road and was now standing, hands on hips, cursing. Gerd was in no mood to enjoy the Stasi man's misfortune. He could only feel it was a missed opportunity. How would he get to talk to her now?

As he watched the beige tram head east out of the city something stopped him. First Miriam had gone to Alexanderplatz, then to the front of the Marienkirche. They were places Miriam and he had met in the last few months. His eyes flashed across to the tram stop.

Gerd smiled to himself. He had a good feeling he knew where Miriam was heading.

***

Miriam passed through the gates of the Volkspark Friedrichshain and headed towards the Marchenbrünnen, the fountain of fairy tales. It was a special place for her; somewhere away from the outside world, untainted and not loaded with the regime's propaganda. She shivered slightly as she headed along the stone sculptures of the fairy tales – Hanzel, Little Red Riding Hood. The dipping sun gave them a creepy quality, yet she was just content to be alone.

She heard the waters of the fountain and felt herself instantly relax. She looked over towards the arches at the back of the fountain, beneath which she'd first kissed him. She felt a warm glow inside. That feeling, the one that came in waves when she thought about Gerd, was the real reason she wanted to leave. She knew now she wanted to be with him. She could understand why her mother thought her to be naïve or not mature enough to make a decision of this magnitude, but she wasn't experiencing what Miriam was feeling. It was a powerful force and she couldn't help being drawn towards it.

She sat on the low wall beside the water. The place was deserted so late in the day and she felt privileged to have the place to herself. Lazily, she put her hand across the surface of the water, breaking her reflection. She laughed; it was only a doe-eyed look anyway. It was the very look Magda told her she had when she talked about Gerd. She took everything in, savouring the smells of the garden and the sounds of the chirping birds as the sun dipped slightly lower in the western sky.

She looked at her watch. Realising she'd been there some time, she thought she'd better make her way back home; no doubt her mother would be fretting that she'd done something stupid. She glanced over towards the arches. She couldn't come to the Marchenbrünnen without standing over there before she left. After all, it was why she had ventured here.

***

He'd watched until the Stasi man had run off to a public phone to report in. He now had his opportunity. He could talk to Miriam unhindered, and he couldn't waste this chance, as it may not occur again. He just hoped he was right about where she was heading.

Gerd retraced his steps to Alexanderplatz and took the tram from there. He didn't alight at the park but one stop before. The last thing he needed was to pick up a tail himself now Miriam was finally alone. He doubled back and eventually headed into the Volkspark from the south side, passing the Grosser Bunkerberg, the man-made hill which contained the ruins of the giant flak tower. He was nervous now, full of anticipation. If he was wrong, or Miriam had already left, he didn't want to think about how bad he would feel. This thought alone made him pick up the pace.

The park was nearly empty, except for the odd person heading home from work in uniform, or with a bag of tools on their back. Gerd was alert to possible tails. When he reached the walkway that led to the fountain, he was almost beside himself. He steadied his breathing in an effort to keep calm. He decided it would be best to approach the fountain from the rear.

He skirted the sculptures close to the tree line. He was so close he could hear the flowing water of the fountain. Finally, he reached the back of the arched stonework. He crept up on one of the archways, keeping low, using one of the giant stone bowls which filled each opening as cover. Holding his breath, he peered down across the water. Aside from the stone figures standing in the stepped pools of the fountain, he couldn't see anybody. He looked again, convinced she would be here, but there was nobody at all.

Gerd sat down, his back perched against the stonework, and sighed deeply. It was here he had first kissed Miriam. He felt certain this was where she would head. He turned again, feeling desperation now, but before he could look properly he heard footsteps heading around the curved archway towards his position. He quickly skipped back towards the tree line. He hid there, his heart beating fast.

First, he saw a long shadow approaching, the low sun peeking through the arches. Then he saw her. He felt elation. He'd been right after all. She continued to walk towards his hiding place. He hesitated. His mind told him to wait and see if she'd been followed, but he knew that was unlikely.

He moved out from his covered position and leant against the stonework. She'd not yet seen him as she peered through the opening.

'You took your time,' he said.

She froze, no doubt wondering if she'd actually heard his voice. She turned to him. There were no more than a couple of metres between them. To Gerd, time felt like it had stopped. Miriam ran towards him, throwing her arms around him.

'How did you…?'

He put his finger to his lips, then he kissed her, slowly. It was different to their last kiss here, more passionate, more needy. He'd found her at last.

***

They talked for a long time. He had to get all the instructions across to her. It wasn't easy in such an emotional moment. Ulrich had emphasised that the important things were the passwords for the courier contact. They had to be dealt with before anything else.

'I'm so sorry I told Magda what I did. Was it bad for you?' Miriam said.

'They arrested me at the checkpoint the last time we met, but I've got it worked out.'

Miriam looked confused for a moment. 'You came to some kind of arrangement?'

Gerd sighed. 'We don't have time to go through it all now. You are being followed.' She went to say something, but he cut her off. 'All you have to do is carry on as normal. Do all the things you would normally do and wait for the contact to come. You have the passwords, so you know who to trust.'

She shook her head. 'I've brought you so much trouble.'

He laughed. 'You have… but you're worth it.'

She smiled, then looked behind her. 'How do you know there's nobody here now?'

'You lost him when you ran for the tram close to the Rotes Rathaus.'

She was amazed. 'You were there then?'

'I was trying to talk to you at the church, but you'd already gone when I reached the front of the building.'

'All this must have been terrible for you.'

'It's done now.' He looked at her intently, gripping her shoulders. 'It's vital you stay calm and go on as normal.'

She nodded. He sensed she'd grown stronger herself over the last few weeks.

He paused, desperate for reassurance of her intentions. 'It won't be over in a short time. It may even take a few months. You know that?'

She nodded quickly. 'It'll be as long as it takes. Don't worry about me.'

'Are you sure you want to do this?' he whispered.

She looked at him now, eyes burning. 'I've never been more certain.'

Gerd felt like a heavy weight had been lifted from his chest. In all those days, in all the things he suffered, Hohenschönhausen, rejection by his friends, he still hadn't been entirely sure Miriam wanted to come west. Now he knew.

'What about your mother?'

'She knows, Gerd.'

He was shocked. 'You told her?'

She was nodding now. 'That I'm in love with you and I want to leave.'

He was surprised she was so forthright. He felt ecstatic, so much so he couldn't speak for a moment.

'That's okay, right? It's what I feel.'

He studied her. It seemed that little girl of two weeks ago had vanished, and here in front of him was a young woman speaking with conviction.

He smiled. He felt tears in his eyes. 'Right now, I don't think I could be any happier, Miriam.'

CHAPTER 31

JULY 1962, WEST BERLIN

The atmosphere in the small side room of Schöneberg town hall was tense. In spite of his assertion he wouldn't get involved in the detail, Ulrich had organised the room and was now making the introductions. Jack had Harry on standby, knowing he had other points to deal with first, and trusting his friend could stay sober long enough.

Sitting opposite Jack and Ulrich were three men. Wilhelm was very young, early twenties, studious-looking with round glasses and a thin face. Accompanying him were a Spaniard, by the name of Pablo. He was older than Wilhelm, in his thirties, tall, languid and calm. Next to him was the small, wiry Italian, Renzo. He was different again, irascible, demonstrative, threatening to erupt like Etna before proceedings really got going. Jack suspected the names were false, but their mistrust was not.

'Gentlemen, thank you for coming here,' Ulrich started. 'Given our previous discussions, I thought you might be interested in what my colleague has to say.'

There wasn't a word; three sets of eyes shifted from Ulrich to Jack. Pablo puffed a plume of smoke above his head, which Renzo wafted away in irritation. Jack felt like the gate had been lifted and he'd been pushed out into the gladiators' arena.

'I haven't come here to waste anybody's time, so let's get down to business.' Jack was about to speak again only to be interrupted as Wilhelm started to translate to the others in English. Pablo continued to stare at him, so Jack guessed this was for Renzo's benefit only.

Wilhelm turned to Jack and nodded.

Jack sighed. He felt this was going to be a long meeting. 'I want to make you an offer.'

Once again, the words were translated. The Italian's eyes turned back to Jack and narrowed dramatically. Ulrich had told him all three were engineering students at the Free University in the city. He wondered how anybody could cope in Berlin with so little German.

'We could do this in English,' Jack said.

'Then I will need to translate into Spanish,' Wilhelm said, raising his eyebrows.

'We should just go on,' Ulrich said, raising his eyes towards the clock on the wall.

Reluctantly, Jack went on in German. 'I represent a well-known television company who would be interested to follow your project, the excavation, the people, and then...' Jack paused, 'the escapes.'

Wilhelm started to translate but Renzo waved him down, as if swatting a fly. He turned to Jack and said, '50,000 dollars.' All of a sudden, his German was pretty good.

'Up front,' Pablo added.

Wilhelm smiled and shrugged.

Jack turned to look at Ulrich, recalling his warnings about their ruthlessness. He'd seen it first-hand now. He had a feeling they were chancing their arm, throwing a wild figure out there, testing the response.

The clock ticking filled the silence.

'That's a steep price,' Jack said.

The Italian shrugged, like he couldn't care less. Pablo lit another cigarette, then said, 'It'll be worth every cent.'

Jack waited. Wilhelm scraped his chair on the wooden floor. The room felt stuffy. Jack looked towards the window and wished he'd opened it before they started. 'That's not a figure we can get anywhere near.'

Wilhelm turned to Pablo. He was seemingly the leader. The Spaniard reached forward to tap ash into the foil tray before him. 'We won't accept less than 40,000.'

Jack pursed his lips, then raised his eyebrows. He wasn't confident. 'I will see what I can do on that. I do have some other conditions.'

The Italian threw his arms up in the air, his understanding of the language now seemingly heightened.

Pablo's eyes narrowed slowly. 'Conditions?'

'I want you to get two people out for me.'

A stream of fast Italian flew from Renzo's lips like hot lava, whilst Wilhelm tried to placate him.

'You misunderstand us, Jack,' Pablo said. 'We don't sell places on the escape. That's not how we operate.'

'Yet I'm ready to pay you.'

Pablo shook his head. 'The money is to fund this and future projects for people we choose, people we know.'

'People we trust,' Renzo chipped in, his German improving by the second.

Jack felt it was time for some flattery. 'If this project is as well planned as I believe it to be, you will be bringing out many people. What's two more?'

'It's more a matter of faith,' Pablo said.

Jack shrugged. 'They're on the other side. They know nothing of your project. We only need to inform them at the right time.'

'And if they're already compromised?' Pablo said, turning his palms to the ceiling.

Renzo was still yattering on to Wilhelm, who was nodding in response.

'I don't believe this can work, Jack,' Pablo said, stubbing out his cigarette in a valedictory manner. 'We can talk about the money, but you have to understand security is everything to us.'

Ulrich gave him a knowing look. Jack sighed, sensing a deadlock, then he thought about Gerd and Hans Erdmann; he owed them to keep trying. He thought he'd give it one last shot.

'I can get you help to dig the tunnel. Experienced men.'

For the first time, Pablo looked towards Renzo. Seemingly money was not the only thing they were short of. The Italian was as still as at any time during the meeting, apparently thinking over Jack's last gambit.

Eventually he shook his head. 'I don't like it,' he said in German.

CHAPTER 32

JULY 1962, EAST BERLIN

Treptower Park was resplendent in the sunshine. The two of them walked hand in hand. It had been that way for a few days now. Hans had finally decided the time to tell Hannah the full story had arrived. His mind was settled that he could fully trust her. He was nervous, yet excited. Since the night at Hannah's apartment, they had spent more time together. They'd been for numerous days out and even shared a romantic dinner. He'd been more than happy for her to lean on him during her time of difficulty. According to Hannah, Miriam had seemed calmer recently, and was getting on with her life, which was more than could be said for her mother.

Whilst she'd had to get used to her daughter's decision, Hannah had still been agitated at times, prone to outbursts of anger. That had reduced in the last few days, but she still seemed distracted. Hans had been waiting for his opportunity to talk to her about the possibility of joining Miriam in the west, all of them together. Ultimately, he was worried he was being selfish; it may have suited his wishes to leave, but that didn't mean it was the same for everybody else.

'How's Miriam?' Hans asked, casually feeling his way towards the topic.

'The same as before: strong, set in her mind.'

'It reminds me of somebody.'

She laughed. There had been little of that recently. 'I used to feel like that, but all this has shaken me, I have to admit it.'

They strolled towards the giant granite monument to the Soviet soldier.

'It's only natural, Hannah. A mother is bound to feel let down.'

'I just worry she won't be happy there, then what?' Hannah threw up her arms in frustration.

Hans tried to be diplomatic. 'I'm sure there are good and bad points to both systems. Neither is perfect. I suppose it's about having the choice to decide…'

'You always want what you can't have.'

'It's not that simple, but I know what you mean,' Hans said.

Hannah shook her head. 'I should have done more to prevent it.'

'And if you had, Miriam would have only wanted it more.'

'So, what do you propose I do? Help her plan to leave? Take her to the tunnel myself? How can I do that if I don't believe in what she's doing?'

Hans wanted to say, "Go with her." He wanted to tell her there was a chance for them all to be together.

The enormous monument loomed over them in the near distance as they took the stepped pathway up towards it. Hans felt the subject of their discussion was ironic, taking place as it was directly under the nose of one of most recognisable monuments to socialist power.

'Honestly, I don't know the answer.' He paused before saying, 'You can spend time with her before she goes. Check in your own mind that she has no doubts about what she's doing. Then, in my opinion, you will have to let her go, Hannah. The only other option is to stop her forcibly, and that means…'

'I know what that means,' she snapped. She sighed. 'Look, I'm sorry. I appreciate you helping me like this. I need a sane mind to get me through it.' She stopped and hugged him. His feelings for her had only grown over the last few weeks, finally forcing his suspicions out of the way. He wanted to help her in any way he could, but he still wasn't sure she wanted to hear his preferred option. It would only confuse her further. Yet, if he didn't, he knew he might regret it.

'You know, the night I was shot on the border… the official story wasn't all of it.' He blurted it right out, as if the fear of missing his chance was too much.

'Really?' She sounded unsurprised. They were close to the final steps up to the monument now. 'There were games going on. You hinted as much at the first meeting we had.'

Hans thought about it again. *Was this the time?* He looked up towards the huge soldier on top of its marble pedestal, a child under one arm, a sword in the other. It always made him bristle.

'I was trying to escape, Hannah.'

She continued walking without breaking her stride. Hans stopped. She turned back towards him. 'You think I didn't know?'

He was shocked for a second, then he sprung up to join her. 'They told you?'

'No, you told me. In your manner, that pained look on your face whenever I mention life here.'

Hans couldn't quite believe it. She grabbed hold of his hand. 'Why do you think I felt I could share all this about Miriam with you?'

His heart sank. 'I thought it was because…'

'And I do, Hans. I do love you very much, but on the other hand, if I loved you and your heart was here, in East Berlin, there's no way I would have told you. It wouldn't have been fair to embroil you in it all.'

Now Hans was confused. He should have felt delight. This wonderful woman had just told him she loved him. Yet he couldn't help thinking she was far too smart for him.

They continued to the top in silence, passing a group of schoolchildren being instructed in the virtues of the Soviet soldier by an overenthusiastic teacher. Hans was still trying to take things in.

Finally, they reached the top and looked back down over the memorial and the surrounding gardens; he had to admit, the Russians knew how to do a monument.

He took a quick look around him. Hannah still seemed unfazed, enjoying the sunshine on her face.

'I believe I can get us all out together, Hannah.' She turned to look at him. He said, 'If you want to go, that is.'

His mouth was dry now. He'd been dreading this moment since he'd considered it might be the faintest possibility.

She only smiled and cupped her hand under his cheek. 'I know, Hans. Why do you think I've been in such a dilemma these past days?'

CHAPTER 33

JULY 1962, WEST BERLIN

People milled around the entrance of the Kongresshalle in business attire. Gerd took in the strange arc of the building's structure. It was a bit like a giant eye. Berliners dubbed it "the pregnant oyster". He'd had been back in West Berlin for two days, but he was still feeding off the elation of seeing Miriam again. Whatever else had happened, the bond between them was now cemented; it was just a matter of time before they would be together.

He was amazed how easily Weber had swallowed the information. Ulrich had told him the tunnel had been abandoned due to persistent flooding, yet it provided Gerd credibility with Weber. Inside the tunnel was information which may, or may not, have thrown Weber off the scent. Intelligence was as much about misinformation as it was about information, Ulrich had explained to him.

Gerd sat by the water feature at the front of the hall. Jack had called him at his uncle's place to meet him. Gerd hoped it meant there had been developments. He'd been waiting a short time before Jack bustled towards him, yanking off his tie.

'Jesus, I hate these dull exhibitions,' Jack moaned.

'I must admit, it sounds a bit boring compared to what you normally cover,' Gerd teased.

'Yeah, well, it pays the bills.' Jack motioned over the road towards the trees of the Tiergarten. 'Come on, let's walk.'

As they reached the park, Gerd couldn't wait. 'So, what's the news, Jack?'

He sighed. 'Not great, I'm afraid.'

Gerd felt his heart drop.

Jack saw the change in his demeanour. 'Look, we've found a tunnel.'

'We?'

'Ulrich and me.'

Gerd stopped. 'You've spoken to Ulrich?'

'It's fine. I didn't tell him anything, not that you told me, but it's okay. We've past that.'

'What are you talking about, Jack?'

'There's an ongoing tunnel project. Some students from the FU. We met them yesterday and talked about you joining them.'

Gerd was sceptical. 'Why would they agree to that?'

'Because I have something to offer them.'

'Like what?'

'A TV contract.'

'What, like the movie?' Gerd said.

Tunnel 28 was a movie re-enacting a real tunnel escape, being shot close by. Even a replica of the wall had been erected on the other side of the Tiergarten. It was big news in the city.

'Yeah, but very real.'

'Let me guess,' Gerd said. 'They didn't like it.'

Jack was quiet for a moment. 'I told them I wanted a place for Miriam on the escape and you on their team.'

'That would be ideal.' Gerd preferred to be doing something rather than hanging around waiting.

'Unfortunately, they're a suspicious bunch.'

Gerd shrugged. 'I'm not surprised.' He thought about his own experiences with Walther and the others. 'Money doesn't buy loyalty, Jack.'

'Christ, you sound like Ulrich.'

Gerd felt resigned, but knew Jack had done his best. 'Well, thanks for trying at least.'

'I'm not giving up yet. It's going to take time, but I'll let you know what happens. I've a feeling they'll be back.'

Gerd had his doubts. He could only think about Miriam and how far away she felt.

'What are you going to do in the meantime?' Jack asked. Gerd could see he was worried about him.

'I'll keep busy, you know me.' He knew he had to hang in there. Something might well turn up. 'I was toying with the idea of going back to talk to Walther. Maybe he can put me in touch with somebody else.'

Jack stopped dead still, his face serious. 'You haven't heard?'

'Heard what?'

'Last night, near Kiefholzstrasse, they took him, Gerd. The Stasi have got Walther.'

CHAPTER 34

AUGUST 1962, WEST BERLIN

Jack parked the Karmann Ghia on Kochstrasse. He was meeting an old friend, a photographer he'd worked with in the past. For once he was early, so he decided to walk around to Friedrichstrasse, close to the checkpoint. Last year, he'd got to know many of the US army personnel, especially after spending so much time there during the standoff with the Soviets. There were no tanks facing each other today, but things had been no less tense. Over the last few days there had been many protests in West Berlin. The Vopos and Schupos had even exchanged tear gas volleys at times. For now, things remained in check. Just.

The intervening weeks had proved difficult. Whilst he was waiting for news, Jack had been busy working on pieces for the anniversary of the division of the city. Gerd had been calling at his apartment almost daily to check for any change. There hadn't been any. Pablo and his suspicious team of tunnellers had not returned, and privately, Jack was beginning to wonder if they ever would.

As Jack approached the white wooden cabin of the US checkpoint, sandbags stacked by the doorway, he heard a shout from across the road.

'Jack!'

Wolfgang Huhn walked over to join him, the obligatory Leica camera hanging around his neck.

'How did I know I'd find you here?'

'You know me, Jack.' He nodded back towards the photography shop. 'Just stocking up on film.'

Jack had worked with him on an assignment with *Newsweek*, but Wolfgang was normally very much freelance. He patrolled up and down the wall, trying to catch the drama, and so far, he'd managed to do plenty of that.

'It just so happens I wanted to talk to you about a project,' Jack said.

They were on the pavement, near the old tobacco shop, within spitting distance of the border line. Wolfgang had his camera in hand, sizing up shots of the East German border guards.

'Sounds interesting,' he said, as the camera clicked. 'Light's not great today.'

Jack looked up at the grey sky. *At least the rain has stopped*, he thought.

'Come on, I'll buy you that coffee and we can talk about it.'

Jack had always had Wolfgang in mind when talking to the tunnellers. Still photo shoots would not have the impact of a live film, but Jack knew there was nobody better in the business to capture the mood in a photograph. The fact Jack didn't have an agreement in place was immaterial. He would need to be in a position to move quickly when he did.

They turned to head back down Friedrichstrasse, away from the border, when they heard gunshots. Jack looked across to see the US guards readying weapons. The shots had come from the direction of the wall.

There was no hesitation from Wolfgang. He headed at a sprint past the US checkpoint. There were more shots.

'Where's it coming from?' Jack shouted at nobody in particular.

Wolfgang was already past the tobacco shop and heading towards the wall to the right of the checkpoint. Faces looked down on Zimmerstrasse from the *Neue Zeit* newspaper building on the eastern side of the wall. They were looking to their left.

'Charlottenstrasse,' Wolfgang shouted on the run.

Jack followed him through the overgrown weeds along the breeze block wall. Past Charlottenstrasse, which was dissected by the wall, a small group of people had gathered beside a US army jeep. Wolfgang was already at the group, asking questions.

Out of breath, Jack finally caught up.

'Escapers,' Wolfgang said. He nodded over to the jeep where a young man sat, a blanket around his shoulders, scratches on his face. The youth looked in shock, his eyes wide, his shoulders shaking. There was a verbal volley of orders from the US sergeant and the jeep sped away from the border area.

'Find me a ladder. Quickly!' Wolfgang was talking to Jack.

Jack looked to the wall some five metres in front of them. The windows of the building directly behind it were boarded or bricked up at ground level.

'What do you want a ladder for?' Then Jack heard the faint voice.

'Help me! Help me!'

One of the buildings in the East was still an apartment block. Three floors up, an older woman stood at the window, her hand over her face. She looked sick with horror. She caught Jack's eye and pointed down to the wall below her, then she disappeared behind the curtains.

Wolfgang had borrowed a short ladder from a fire truck which had appeared. 'Come on!' he shouted.

'Are you mad? They're firing real bullets, Wolfgang.' Jack shook his head and followed his friend at a low run. He certainly didn't feel like taking a bullet for a good photograph.

They were at the wall now and the cries of the man below were much clearer. 'Why aren't you helping me?'

Jack put the ladder against the wall. Wolfgang was up it and pushing the barbed wire aside. He cursed as he tried to force his camera through the wire. Jack looked back towards the gathering of people, which was growing, although nobody seemed to be doing anything to help the injured man.

Above Jack, Wolfgang was cursing, but nonetheless his camera was whirring away, shot after shot.

'He's bleeding badly. Go get help!' Wolfgang shouted, seemingly not intent on moving himself.

The US troops had left the scene. There were a variety of onlookers, mainly ordinary Berliners, hurling insults at the East German border guards, but nobody was doing anything to organise a retrieval mission.

Jack left Wolfgang to his snapping and returned to the swelling crowd. 'Has anybody called an ambulance?' A Schupo stood as if frozen in shock. Jack grabbed him. 'That boy is bleeding to death! Can't you do something to help him?'

'The Amis could do something. They've taken the other one away,' he said defensively.

Jack cursed and sprinted off back towards the checkpoint. He knew in his professional capacity he should be already calling in the story, but his human side had been deeply affected by the young man's cries. He ran on past some people climbing the wooden steps of the platform, trying to get a better view of the unfolding drama.

At Checkpoint Charlie, the Americans were looking back in the direction from where Jack had come.

'Somebody's lying on the other side of the wall. He's been shot. If we don't get help, he'll die,' Jack managed through his panting.

The guard was fresh-faced and slightly overawed by the whole thing. He didn't say anything but ran over to the army office next to the tobacco shop. A young officer was already on the phone.

'Are you sure?' he said down the line.

He put down the telephone, his face drained of colour.

Jack pushed his way in front of the young guard. 'You have to organise some help. A man is bleeding to death over there!'

The officer wiped his sleeve across his mouth. 'We've been ordered to provide assistance, but not to step foot on the Eastern side.'

Jack was incredulous. 'You've got guns to protect yourselves. Go over, get him out. He'll be dead if you do nothing.'

The officer shrugged. 'He's on the Eastern side. I've just been told, "It's not our problem."'

***

Jack was weary. He flopped onto the couch, whisky in hand. The place was silent; Eva and Tanja were in bed long ago, but there was a ringing in his ears, the tension of the day still coursing through his veins. Professionally, the day could not have been any better. He'd persuaded Wolfgang to give his employers first refusal on the photographs. He'd filed the story. His bosses at *Newsweek* would be happy at least. The story had to be told, the pictures to be published, yet the whole thing made Jack sick to the core.

The young man had died at the foot of the wall, his body eventually manhandled away by East German border guards under a pathetically inadequate smokescreen. There was no hiding what had happened. Jack expected callous behaviour and lies from Ulbricht and his mob, but the inaction on the Western side, from his own countrymen, was unforgiveable. He knew the Americans didn't want to cause an incident by stepping foot on East German soil, even though army helicopters could fly overhead providing cover, if required.

The whole episode didn't reflect well on anybody. The world had stood by whilst a young man bled to death in the middle of a major European city. Even as a hardened journalist and a war veteran, Jack knew brutal wasn't enough to describe the scene. He drank even though the warmth of the whisky flowing down his chest was not enough to soothe his mind. If he hadn't known before, he knew now this would not end. Positions had just become more entrenched. The message to Ulbricht was very clear: what happens on your side of the line is your business. The East Germans would kill in full view without compunction, the West Berliners would stand on, angry yet helpless whilst the Western allies did nothing. One year on from the division of the city, the lines had been well and truly drawn.

Eventually, his breathing slowed and deepened. It was the toss of a coin between the warmth of his bed and the consoling tones of another VAT 69. The weariness in his body reflected his feelings for the city. He wondered how Gerd had received the news. He hoped it didn't make him feel as desperate as the two young men who'd thrown themselves at the wall today. One had succeeded by the skin of his teeth; his friend died in a pool of his own blood, calling for help.

The telephone rang, and Jack looked up to the ceiling in anguish. He thought about letting it ring out, but answered it, worried Tanja and Eva might be disturbed.

'Kaymer.'

'Jack, it's Ulrich.'

'Tell me something to cheer me up.'

'Tough day?'

'I was down at the wall on Zimmerstrasse today. The dead kid.'

'Ah,' Ulrich said. 'Not good.'

There was a silence, as if a moment of respect was called for.

'So, any good news?' Jack said finally.

'It's back on, Jack. The Spaniard just called me.'

Jack sighed. There was a god after all. 'When?'

'Tomorrow morning. Can you get the TV guy there?'

Jack's heart sank. He'd forgotten about Harry.

CHAPTER 35

AUGUST 1962, WEST BERLIN

Gerd was standing close to the wall on Zimmerstrasse. There were flowers and heartfelt messages of condolence and support, but they couldn't overcome the anger felt in the city. By now it was known locally the dead man was Peter Fechter. He'd been two years older than Gerd. Gerd hadn't known him or his friend, the one who managed to escape, but he knew many more like them.

He shared the anger of other Berliners. There had been demonstrations the previous night, and, looking around him, he felt another brewing today. They despised the border guards and their hated actions in shooting on fellow Germans. It was, however, the first time he'd heard such open hatred of the Americans. Before there was resentment and the odd spiteful word but this was different. Things had changed.

His own outrage was very much channelled, however. He'd since heard of the details of Walther's arrest. Kiefholzstrasse had been another botched operation; when they appeared in the basement of a house on the other side of the border, the Stasi had been lying in wait. Unlike on Heidelberger Strasse, this time Walther had been captured. Gerd had heard the tale from an apologetic Jürgen, who'd escaped with seconds to spare. This time, Arno had disappeared. They had drawn their own conclusions and Gerd had been exonerated over the Heidelberger Strasse fiasco. His instinct had been correct. He didn't hold any grudges, but he felt for Walther.

He'd been tempted to go back to the Girmann organisation building and offer his services once more, but Ulrich had cautioned against it.

Ulrich didn't say why, but Gerd suspected he knew their organisation had been compromised by Stasi agents; probably Arno wasn't the only one. Ulrich rarely explained why, but Gerd was learning to follow his cautious, yet meticulous, approach. For Gerd, it was just about maintaining patience and waiting for the opportunity. The only other way was to start his own project, but he needed funds to do that.

His focus returned to the growing number of tributes to the dead man. He looked towards the wall, silently cursing the misery it had brought. He thought about Miriam and closed his eyes. He was determined nobody would be leaving flowers at his memorial. He had to get it right, and he was trusting Jack and Ulrich to come through for him.

***

Harry's apartment was on Fasanenstrasse. For his lifestyle it was the right place, close to the bright lights of the Ku'damm. He could only hope that he'd managed to hang on in Berlin by convincing Ricksen he had something of substance. His apartment was paid for by the TV company and came with a landlady who cooked for residents and kept the place in order. She was house-proud type which, unfortunately for her, didn't exactly fit with having somebody like Harry around.

Jack was at least relieved that the landlady confirmed Harry was still there. She was in her late fifties, severe looking without the furrowed brow; with it, she was downright intimidating.

'Herr O'Donnell was late back *again* this morning.' She raised her eyebrows as if Jack had something to do with it.

'I just need to talk to him,' Jack said.

She scoffed. 'You'll be lucky.' She turned and banged on his door. Her thudding rocked the place. It must have been impossible for anybody to sleep through it. 'Herr O'Donnell, there is somebody to see you.'

They waited together through an awkward silence, anticipating a sign of life from inside. It was just enough time for her to give Jack a disdainful once-over. Jack had heard about the dreaded *Blockwarte* of the Nazi period. This woman must have been a descendent.

She started banging again, which led Jack to step back.

'Perhaps you have a key?' he offered.

Suddenly her face was full of virtue. 'You don't believe I can just walk into a guest's apartment on a whim, Herr…?'

'Kaymer,' Jack said with a sigh. 'Maybe you could make an exception just this once?' Jack's smile was returned with a cold scowl.

Jack thought flattery might be worth a shot. 'You must be very busy keeping this place in tip-top condition, *Fräulein*.'

She smiled. It could have frozen a polar bear, but Jack felt he was getting somewhere. 'Frau Schwarz,' she said, still smiling.

She thought about it for a split second, then produced a bunch of keys of which a jailer would have been proud, and found the relevant key in an instant.

The stench of stale alcohol hit them first. '*Mein Gott!*' Her face was screwed up as if she were sucking a lemon. Frau Schwarz was across the room, flinging open the window, before she could see what Jack was laughing at.

A very pale backside stared back at them. The landlady shrieked and was out of the room in a flash. 'I'll leave it to you, Herr Kaymer,' she called, from the safety of the hallway.

'Perhaps you'd be kind enough to fetch me a bucket of water,' Jack said, laughing to himself.

Harry was somewhere in the heap of sheets; the backside testified to that. By the smell of the room it had been a good night; another one. Jack wondered how many there had been since he'd saved him that night at the Eden more than a month ago. He was starting to think somebody didn't want him to help Gerd and Hans Erdmann, but he'd come this far, and Jack wasn't about to give up.

He heard the bucket being placed in the doorway. 'Please don't make a mess, Herr Kaymer.'

Jack looked around the place. Clothes were strewn everywhere. Papers and books were stacked around and on top of two typewriters that looked like they'd been unused for some time. Empty whisky bottles were piled high on both sides of the bed. What he did with the water wasn't going to make the slightest difference to the state of the room.

He tried to shake Harry out of his deep slumber. He was like the immovable object.

Jack shook his head. He didn't have time to waste. He picked up the pail, stepping back so he didn't get wet, and launched the contents over Harry and the bed.

*****

Jack had finally levered Harry O'Donnell out of his mangy pit and had him installed close by with the TV company's cheque book in his pocket. It didn't suit Jack to have Harry part of the discussion, if he could manage it himself. It didn't help Harry wasn't up to it, but he also wasn't aware of Jack's conditions. He had used Harry's tab at the Kempinski to hire a room, and informed Ulrich of the venue. Jack's unstable business partner waited in the café downstairs with instructions to the staff to provide nothing but strong coffee.

The room turned out to be a suite, one of the best in the hotel, normally reserved for the company's top executives. There was no doubting the resources at Harry's fingertips.

The Spaniard, Pablo, arrived first and shook Jack's hand without a word. He looked around and raised an eyebrow. Why did Jack get the feeling the price had just increased?

'Privacy is important for the project,' Jack said quickly.

The Italian, Renzo, arrived with Wilhelm, and took the liberty of checking every corner of the place before he felt ready to talk.

The atmosphere was as tense as at their previous meeting, so much so Jack was glad when Ulrich finally arrived.

Once they were around the table, Ulrich took up the lead. 'Gentlemen, you indicated a willingness to talk?'

They all looked to Pablo. There was no pretence of translation this time. In fact, Jack wondered why Wilhelm was there.

'Things have changed recently,' he said, before lighting up a cigarette.

Ulrich had told Jack the tunnel had sprung a leak a couple of weeks before. Maybe this was the reason for their change of heart.

'Yesterday's events rather focused our minds,' the Spaniard added in explanation. Renzo nodded sternly at his side.

Was this really about outrage at the Fechter killing, or was it just a way of making their negotiating position appear less weak? Jack didn't buy it, but why they were here was really only important to the price; the fact they were meant there was a deal to be done.

'I seem to recall the conditions were the issue last time,' Jack said. There was no point in wasting time. Renzo glared at him, then at Ulrich.

'We'll get to that,' Pablo said. 'We want 20,000 dollars for the film.'

Ulrich turned to Jack. The price had halved since their last demand.

Jack sensed the tide had changed. If they were back at the table, it was because the men in front of Jack needed to be there. It also meant they would accept his conditions, otherwise they wouldn't have come.

'The best I can do is 10,000.'

There were sharp intakes of breath all round, yet Pablo remained calm, smooth. 'Don't think for a minute this money is for the people around the table. This is about funding this and future projects.' He pointed his cigarette whilst he made his point.

'Your motives are not my concern,' Jack said. Ulrich gave him a sharp look.

Jack wasn't concerned. He knew how cultures worked, especially when it came to negotiation. The south European way wasn't the same as the north. As if to mirror his thoughts, Jack looked across at the German, Wilhelm, meek and stiff, at the periphery.

'Our last price is 15,000,' the Spaniard said.

Jack stared back at Pablo. He had a lazy eye which extenuated his already relaxed nature.

'Difficult,' Jack said finally.

Renzo stood up, apparently ready to leave.

Jack held up his hand, worrying he'd pushed it too far. 'But perhaps I can get close to it,' Jack said.

Pablo nodded for his friend to sit down. The Italian gave Jack a condescending look and retook his seat. Wilhelm seemed embarrassed. Ulrich inspected his nails, as if he'd heard it all before.

'What about my requests?' Jack said.

Here Ulrich intervened. 'The help has been BfV interrogated. I can vouch for him personally.'

It was Jack's turn to be impressed. He always thought Ulrich worked for the BND. He wondered where the domestic security service, state security and foreign intelligence crossed paths. Whatever the case, it seemed Gerd had been vetted and given the all clear.

Renzo leant over to say something to Pablo. 'Okay, we can use the help,' the Spaniard said.

'What about my places on the escape?'

'They are yours,' Pablo said.

Jack smiled, scenting victory.

'However,' Pablo pulled hard on his cigarette, then blew a plume of blue-grey smoke above his head, 'they will only be given details of the meeting point after all the other people are through the tunnel. And that is non-negotiable.'

Jack sighed. He could understand the need for security. After all, these men had done all the work; it was only right that their family and friends should be the first ones out. They shouldn't be put at risk by people they didn't know.

'Okay. Agreed.'

'As for the fee,' Pablo smiled for the very first time, 'I am sure your own employers could help with that, Herr Kaymer.'

Jack looked at Ulrich, who just shrugged.

'You don't believe we wouldn't have you checked out. You have had some nice scoops in the past, no?'

Renzo crossed his arms and smiled smugly.

'What about 12,000 from the TV company, 2,000 from *Newsweek*?' Jack said, disappointed he couldn't keep the *Newsweek* part until later in the negotiation. Sometimes his name preceded him.

The room was quiet now, each of them knowing they were close to the final agreement, but not quite there.

Pablo shrugged, seemingly undecided.

'I know a very good photographer, the best. Wolfgang Huhn, maybe you have heard of him?' Jack said.

Pablo nodded. 'His photos are all over the papers today.'

Jack nodded, his point made. 'I'm sure his skills, and name, will earn you the extra you require.'

Pablo turned to Renzo, who, after a dramatic pause, gave a nonchalant shrug.

The Spaniard leant forward, offering his hand. 'Okay, Herr Kaymer, you've got a deal. Shall we go and look at the tunnel?'

CHAPTER 36

AUGUST 1962, EAST/WEST BERLIN

As Hans Erdmann waited on the Lustgarten, he felt a mixture of emotions. He was still wondering how Hannah could work so much out without being given what he felt was the slightest inkling. He was supposed to be the one trained and experienced in the game of espionage; maybe he was losing his touch. Then again, he had come to realise there was one factor he'd never had to contend with during his time working for Burzin; his love for Hannah had inhibited the normal, rational functioning of his mind. That wasn't going to stop any time soon; in fact, it would only grow. For the first time the previous night, they'd shared a bed, and Hans only wanted more.

He was behind the Berliner Dom, facing onto the Spree river. He turned to see Hannah coming towards him. How her mannerisms had changed since that first day they'd walked together on the Lustgarten. He knew the stresses of this uncertain world very well; he'd been here before. His eyes scanned the scene behind her, looking for anything suspicious, out of place. There was good reason for that.

She kissed him, her hand slipping behind his head.

'It's so hard to concentrate on work,' she said.

'I have that effect on women.'

She laughed. 'It would be nice if that was the only thing on my mind.'

He glanced over towards the wooden footbridge which had replaced the blown-up Friedrichsbrücke at the end of the war, then turned and led her towards the very back of the cathedral.

'I find it hard to look my colleagues in the eye, Hans.'

He sighed, thinking back to the previous August. He recalled the feeling. In fact, since he'd been transferred to Berlin he'd been constantly hiding something from someone. 'It gets easier in time,' he said.

'Sometimes I think they can see straight through me.'

'Probably the only thing they might be able to see is that you're not yourself. Yet I am sure you are different at work to how you are at home.'

'Maybe,' she said thoughtfully.

The decision was easy for Hans. The only person he had really cared about at the time of his escape attempt had been Bernie. He was at least now safe in the west and Hans took comfort from that. He knew the dilemma in Hannah's mind. It was different for her. Her whole outlook on life held so much more in common with the policies of the DDR than with those of the capitalist West. Hans knew she was a very principled woman. In fact, it was one of the things that attracted him.

'I often wonder what I would even do over there.'

'What you do now.' It was obvious to Hans.

'And what will you do? You won't walk into the Bundeswehr with your record,' she joked.

Hans laughed. 'It wasn't exactly my intention.'

She turned to him, biting her lip. He'd never seen her do that before. It gave her a vulnerable air, one he felt he needed to put his arm around and protect from the world, even though he doubted Hannah would appreciate the sentiment.

'How long do you need... to plan, I mean?'

He shrugged. 'It will just be about opportunity. Papers. Maybe even a tunnel, like Miriam.'

'If I decide to go through with this, I would feel better if we all went together.'

'Naturally,' Hans said, doing his best to suppress the elation he was feeling inside.

'I have to warn you, though, it's by no means decided I will go. Everything I believe in is here. I can't begin to imagine how I would feel over there.'

The warning was stark, and it brought Hans back down from his fluffy cloud with a hefty thump. He held back from trying to persuade her. She wasn't the type to react too well to being pushed in any way. It had to be her decision, because, he knew, that was the only way she would come to terms with her new life.

'Take your time. It's not a decision to be made hastily.'

She smiled, hugging him close. 'I'm so glad you're here, Hans. I don't know what I'd do without you.'

He sighed, knowing he'd felt like that about her almost from the beginning.

He was maintaining a watch on the people around them. Workmen were discarding waste at the side of the Altesmuseum. They were laughing and joking with each other. At least somebody was in good spirits.

'There is something we have to deal with more urgently,' he said.

She took her head from his chest. 'Such as?'

'We need to talk to Miriam.'

'We?'

Hans nodded.

When he'd arrived at Hannah's apartment the previous evening, as a precaution, he'd spent some time reconnoitring the area before he finally entered the apartment by a rear route.

'Don't you think it's too early? I haven't decided what I will do yet.'

'It's not about that, Hannah.'

'Then what?'

'The Stasi. Last night, they were outside your apartment. Miriam is under surveillance.'

***

Jack's news had thrilled Gerd. At last, the good news he'd been praying for had finally arrived. The tunnellers Jack had previously spoken to had returned to the negotiating table and thrashed out a deal. Jack had even been to see the tunnel. Ulrich had already arranged to get a message to Miriam. Now Gerd had to meet the project team before they were to start work together under more pressing circumstances. Gerd had only been too eager to agree.

'Just try and stay calm,' Jack said, as they waited at his apartment. 'I'm sure you'll get along just fine.'

Gerd shrugged. 'I think you're more nervous than me.' It was bravado, but somehow it felt right to say it.

The noise of the door buzzer made Gerd flinch. Jack laughed. 'Not nervous, eh?'

Gerd pulled a face, motioning Jack towards the door.

There were two of them: a tall man with a thatch of dark, swept-back hair, and a smaller guy, wiry, agile. *Made for digging tunnels*, Gerd thought.

Jack made the introductions. 'Gerd, this is Pablo.' He shook hands with the tall one, who half-smiled. 'And Renzo.' This one had an iron grip and an intense stare.

'Shall we take a seat?' Jack said, winking to Gerd when the others weren't watching.

'May I?' Pablo looked to Jack, gesturing with a pack of cigarettes. Jack handed him an ash tray.

Renzo was still eyeing Gerd, making him feel slightly uncomfortable, even though he was doing his best not to show it. 'Herr Kaymer said you have tunnelling experience.'

Gerd swallowed. He'd been worried about this question from the beginning. The *Fluchthelfer* community was relatively small and close-knit. Whatever he said could be checked out in one or two calls. Gerd just hoped Arno's deception, and Gerd's subsequent vindication, had already hit the grapevine.

'I worked with Walther Noltke on two different projects, but mainly on the last one on Heidelberger Strasse.'

'The one from the pub?' Pablo asked.

Renzo glanced across at Pablo. 'How well do you know Noltke?'

'Since I was a kid…'

'Then you must be Gerd Braun,' Renzo said.

Gerd's heart sank. The room was silent. They knew his name. Even Jack looked worried.

Gerd only nodded.

Pablo blew a plume of smoke out in front of him. 'We're sorry to hear about your friend. A fine man.'

Renzo was nodding next to him. Then he smiled for the first time.

'He is,' Gerd said.

Gerd had a feeling they knew everything about him already. The first questions were only a test, to see if he what he said added up.

'In fact, he mentioned you. He even speaks highly of you,' Renzo said.

'You've seen him recently? I mean before…'

Renzo looked towards Pablo, who gave a small but discernible nod. 'We helped them on Kiefholzstrasse.'

'Right,' Gerd said, glancing nervously at Jack.

'There were one or two problems on our project, all fixed now, but we were able to help them in the meantime,' Pablo explained. 'A special request from Girmann.'

Gerd raised his eyebrows; their contacts were impressive.

'Not that it did much good.' Renzo's scowl was dark and threatening. 'You knew this Arno?' He spat the name. Gerd could only grimace. 'You already suspected him?'

Gerd shook his head. 'I had no real proof. I talked to Walther about my suspicions, but he wanted to push on…'

'Yet this Arno tried to blame you for the Heidelberger Strasse tunnel.' His eyes pierced him, but Gerd didn't mind now. He understood the need to ask these questions. After his own experiences, Gerd would certainly have done the same. More than that, it gave Gerd confidence in them and their project. As much as he admired Walther, his downfall was his inability to do this "dirty" part of the job.

'When things go wrong you have to find out why,' Gerd said. 'That needs a level head and rational thinking. In that situation, the *Spitzel* Arno was shouting the loudest.'

'He's a dead man if I set eyes on him again,' Renzo said. Gerd didn't have reason to doubt him.

'That's not likely to happen.' Pablo was trying to lighten the mood a little. 'So, you know how to dig, you're not scared of hard work, and it seems you have people vouching for you, people who we trust. What do you say, Renzo?'

The Italian was scowling, but Gerd had come to realise that was his resting expression. Quickly it changed to a full-beamed smile. He looked directly at Gerd. 'You'll do for us,' he said, finally.

Laughter broke out in the room; for Gerd it was more relief than anything.

'We should go and look at the tunnel now,' Pablo said. 'I think it will be different from anything you've been used to before.'

***

It was the last thing Miriam had expected. At first, she'd been angry with her mother for telling him. She no longer suspected the man was spying on her, as had been her initial paranoia at the beach, but still, her mother had gone too far in telling Hans Erdmann she planned to escape West. How could she trust this man? He worked for the government, upholding the laws of the DDR. What if he now decided to denounce her, or even her mother? It had taken a lot of hard talking from her mother to get her to listen. Miriam did wonder if she'd been blinded by her feelings for the man, but in the end, Miriam did agree to talk to him.

They were sat in the apartment at the small dining table, her mother watching over her. Miriam had her arms crossed in front of her. She was prepared to listen to the man, but she didn't have to like what he had to say.

'I'm glad you agreed to talk to me, Miriam.' He smiled. She could understand why her mother liked him; he was warm and good-looking in a distinguished sort of way, but that didn't mean he was to be trusted.

She only nodded tersely.

'I realise you might be suspicious of me and my intentions. I would be the same in your shoes, but I do only want what is best for you and your mother.'

Miriam raised her eyebrows. She wondered how this man knew what was best for her when he didn't even know her.

'There are things you need to be aware of.'

Miriam sighed. What could this man possibly know that could help her? Gerd had given her the information she needed and how she was to be contacted.

Hans glanced across at her mother. She made a face at Miriam as if she should listen.

'Go ahead,' she said.

'I wonder if you are aware that you're being followed.'

'Yes, I am aware.'

He looked surprised. 'Really?'

'Blonde hair, early thirties. Ridiculous coat for August, always stands by the S-Bahn stop with a newspaper.'

He laughed. It was her mother's turn to look surprised.

'Well, that's good at least. So, it means you'll be keeping your normal routines.'

She nodded. 'I know all this. Gerd told me already.'

'You've seen him?' Her mother was aghast.

The man held up his hand for her mother not to interrupt. 'And you sure you weren't followed when you met him?'

She sighed dramatically. 'Yes. Look, I don't want to appear rude, but I don't know why my mother shared this with you…'

'Miriam!'

'No, Mum.' She turned back to Hans. 'With the greatest respect, I don't know you. You work for the government, one I don't happen to like too much, and you have suddenly appeared on the scene, offering advice…'

'Miriam, please!'

'It's fine, let her finish,' Hans said very calmly.

Miriam nodded, at least grateful the man was prepared to give her a chance to speak.

'Why should I listen to what you tell me? What could you possibly know about my position? How could you put yourself in my shoes?'

The man smiled again. Whatever she had said to him didn't seem to have upset him. 'These are fair questions, Miriam, and I'm not sure I can answer them to your satisfaction, but does it help if I tell you that not so very long ago, I tried to escape through the wire myself?'

CHAPTER 37

AUGUST 1962, WEST BERLIN

Pablo had been right. Gerd hadn't seen a tunnel like this before. When he'd worked with Walther on the other tunnels, there'd been no lights, little ventilation and no wooden supports. Already, the tunnel on Bernauer Strasse was over one hundred metres long. It was fully boarded out, there were lights every five metres, and a large industrial pump filled the tunnel with fresh air. Gerd couldn't help but be impressed.

'This is incredible. People could come through here and not even get dirty.'

'It hasn't always been like this,' Pablo said.

They were in a disused factory, facing onto Bernauer Strasse. Like Heidelberger Strasse, the close proximity of the buildings on either side of the border lent itself to tunnel digging, although Gerd could see the soil which had been excavated was quite different in this part of the city.

'It looks more like clay,' he said.

Renzo nodded. 'The water is high here. We've had many leaks from pipes above, too.'

In the background Harry O'Donnell and his camera crew were setting up for the initial filming. Gerd had heard about the man from Jack, but at least for the moment he seemed sober and working hard with his team to cover their investment. He was constantly asking questions, much to Renzo's ire.

'The man is a pain in the ass,' he hissed to Pablo.

He shrugged. 'We needed the money, my friend. What choice did we have?'

Gerd had quickly been taken into the team's confidence. It seemed they knew a lot about him, which meant they'd taken the time to have him checked out. They were open with him which gave him confidence, not only for himself but in their professionalism and thorough preparation. This was the real thing and he could understand why they were so security conscious. This tunnel, if it maintained its secrecy, could eventually bring hundreds of people out of East Berlin.

Pablo flicked his head at Gerd, taking him to one side. 'As you are aware of all this,' he nodded towards the cameramen, 'you will work when the cameras are here.'

From the scale of the operation, Gerd had quickly realised there must have been up to twenty people digging around the clock. It meant many of the others were not aware of the cameras, nor the money the team had received.

Gerd nodded, then, as an afterthought, added, 'I'd prefer not to be on the film.'

Renzo smiled. 'Your spy friend already informed us you're not to appear on the camera under any circumstances.'

Ulrich was already one step ahead.

'How long before we reach the target site?' Gerd asked.

'Maybe two weeks,' Pablo said.

Gerd held up his hands. 'I don't want to know all the details. I know the trouble it can cause.'

Renzo started to laugh. 'I like your style.' He looked over to Pablo. 'I already like this young man.'

Pablo passed Gerd a small entrenching spade. No matter how developed the structure and how sophisticated the project planning, the old-fashioned graft to dig out the tunnel would always be the same. 'Time to get started.'

There was a clapping of hands behind them. 'Guys, could we get rolling now?' Harry O'Donnell was also impatient to get going.

Renzo visibly bristled at the interruption. Gerd wondered how smooth the filming process would be.

***

Jack could have been relaxed and satisfied; the cards had fallen into place. Gerd was in the tunnel and seemingly getting along well with his fellow tunnellers, and they had secured places for Miriam and Hans Erdmann on the escape run. Yet, in spite of all that, there were still things to be sorted out, matters which were outside his control. Ulrich had given him the nod to initiate contact with Erdmann, and that, of course, meant involving his father-in-law once again. He felt marginally better about that after their parting discussion, but there were still always nagging doubts with Jack where Klaus was concerned.

Jack had tried to get hold of his father-in-law the previous evening without success. He was relieved when he heard his voice.

'Schultz.'

'It's Jack, Klaus.'

There was a pause. 'You can only be ringing for one thing.'

'It's time, Klaus.'

There was a grunt. 'When?'

'Within two weeks.'

Klaus chuckled. 'You got there in the end then?'

'We've not done anything yet.' Jack was doing his best not to let Klaus rile him.

'True enough. I'll get some flights organised.'

'When can you get here?'

'I'm just finishing a job. Day after next.'

'Okay, that's fine.'

'How's the lad?'

'Gerd? Hanging in there,' Jack said.

'He's a tough one.'

It was fine praise indeed from a man like Klaus, but he was right. He wondered if Klaus was in the mood to talk; it wasn't like him to be on the phone any longer than necessary.

'Listen, are you okay with this? There are other ways we can do this if necessary,' Jack said.

There was silence.

'Probably, but they would take too long. It's just… ghosts from the past. It'll be fine.'

Jack knew there were a few, and was sure there were others he didn't know about.

'See you in a couple of days,' Klaus said.

The line went dead.

CHAPTER 38

AUGUST 1962, EAST/WEST BERLIN

Knowing not to leave such things to instinct, Miriam had made her way to the local library in Pankow. If what Erdmann had told her was true, there would at least be newspaper reports about the incident. She couldn't particularly recall it at the time, but there had been so many instances of "border incursions" just after the Russian sector had been sealed off from the rest of the city.

A helpful librarian pointed her in the direction of the back copies of *Neues Deutschland*, and Miriam quickly located the relevant month. She knew it would be after August 13th, as that was when the border was sealed, and possibly a few days on from that when guards continued to establish the border through fences and concrete blocks. She had heard whispered stories of people swimming the Landwehrkanal to escape, or sneaking through the thick trees of the wooded Heidekampgraben in Treptow.

Miriam had been shocked by Hans Erdmann's revelation. This was a colonel in the Volksarmee who was claiming he tried to defect. Was he telling the truth, or was it part of the plan to gain her confidence? She was much more suspicious than she had been just one month ago. She'd learnt not to take anything at face value. That said, she couldn't help liking the man; he seemed genuine and his love for her mother was clear to see. His story would explain why he was prepared to get himself involved in something like this. Any upstanding citizen of the DDR would have reported her and her mother to the authorities, unless, of course, you were planning to escape yourself.

She'd been looking for around an hour when she found the headline in the 18th August edition. "Brave Border Guard Shot by Bandits." The name stood out: Hans Erdmann. She knew that was his real name at least. She quickly skimmed the report, which stated Erdmann had been shot "protecting the border from insurgents". Clearly, the authorities couldn't tell the real story, not Erdmann's version anyway. The question she had was, why would they cover it up? Why hadn't Erdmann been arrested? She felt like she had answered some questions only to reveal more.

She'd been so engrossed in the newspapers, she'd not noticed the man opposite her, reading a book. It was only when he cleared his throat in a particularly irritating way did she look up. Immediately Miriam recognised him as the young man from the hardware shop. He pushed a folded newspaper across the table towards her. She glanced around, checking nobody was watching them.

As casually as she could, she reached for the newspaper. She found a small piece of paper inside. "Mallet" was written on the top. It was the password. She already knew the man from before, but this was confirmation he'd come from Gerd.

She looked up, but the man was already heading towards the door. She read the note.

"Your aunt will arrive within the next two weeks."

Gripped with excitement, she couldn't stop herself from smiling. The escape was on.

***

Gerd Braun was taking a well-earnt rest. He'd been digging at the face for the last three days, resting in between on camp beds on an upper floor of the factory. He was still marvelling at the level of the planning of the project. They'd even tapped into the electricity supply of the factory above them with the consent of the owner. He couldn't help being impressed, yet the scale of the operation worried him. It was much more than he had ever experienced during his time with

Walther, but that meant it had taken more time to plan, to dig, and that meant more people had to have been involved. The more people involved, the more people knew about a part of the project, if not all of it, and this in turn increased the risk of one of those people being in the employ of the Stasi.

He was grateful for the hot coffee, feeling the damp had soaked into his bones somehow. Renzo sat down next to his bed, his back to the wall.

'We're making good progress with your help.'

'How much further?' Gerd asked.

'Maybe another five metres. Three, maybe four days.'

Gerd sighed. He knew Ulrich had sent someone to contact Miriam. He couldn't wait for the whole thing to be over now.

Renzo looked thoughtful. The two of them had grown close over the last few days, working together in such close confines. They'd been paired together because he knew about the filming. The TV crews weren't around when the other tunnellers arrived. Gerd admired Renzo's spirit. Even though the Italian was one of the engineers, he wasn't afraid to get his hands dirty and do his fair share of the work.

'She must be special to you,' Renzo said finally.

Gerd smiled.

'To go through what you've been through, I mean. All that trouble the *Spitzel* caused must not have been easy.'

'She's worth it.'

'What's her name?'

'Miriam,' Gerd said. 'What about you? Why are you doing all this?'

'Not for family. I'm from Trieste. My parents would go mad if they knew the risks I was taking.'

'So why, then?'

'I studied with so many good people. From one day to the next they were denied the right to study in West Berlin.' He turned to Gerd, his eyes intense. 'They are clever people, Gerd, the future of the country, and now, because they dared to want to better themselves, that idiot

Ulbricht makes them sweep the streets. They are punished because they were so-called "border-crossers".'

Gerd had heard so many similar stories. In some ways, Miriam was actually one of the privileged of the DDR, everything mapped out in front of her, if she chose. Yet it would never be a free choice. There would always be compromises, and Gerd was glad she wanted to join him in the West.

'The good thing is, we'll be through soon, then we can help these people to study again, to be with their families again,' Renzo said.

There was a sound of a tool being kicked across the floor. Renzo's eyes narrowed.

'We'll be up on Rheinsberger Strasse before you know it.' His voice was loud, almost as if it were said for somebody else's benefit.

It was then Harry O'Donnell appeared, busily gathering up a microphone lead. He looked up and seemed surprised to see them. 'We're just about finished for today.'

Renzo nodded tersely, then he turned to Gerd, tapping him on the knee. 'Come on, this tunnel won't dig itself.'

CHAPTER 39

AUGUST 1962, WEST/EAST BERLIN

Jack was back at the Café Kranzler. He couldn't believe it had only been two months before that he'd sat here and first recognised the turmoil in Gerd. So much had happened since then and Jack had a feeling the biggest drama was yet to come. The tunnel was nearing completion, but it hadn't been without its hitches, even in the short time Jack had known about it. The sheer number of people involved in the operation worried Jack. It only needed one slip of the tongue in the presence of the wrong person for things to unravel quickly.

Jack waved as he saw Matt Collins dodging the traffic of the Ku'damm. It was so hot even Matt had discarded his suit jacket, though the shirt was pressed to perfection and sunglasses were in place. He was out of breath by the time he got to Jack.

'Busy as ever, Matt?'

He took a seat, shaking his head. 'We're all trying to keep a lid on things at the moment.'

The situation in the city hadn't really improved since the Fechter killing. Jack was constantly reporting on youths peppering border guards with stones, and that often led to exchanges of tear gas between and East and West Berlin police. The Brits had even had to put a perimeter guard on the Soviet monument close to the Reichstag. For a number of days, the bus transporting the Soviet soldiers to the monument had been showered with bricks, breaking windows and threatening a diplomatic flare-up. The place was the next crisis away from tipping point.

'There's always something going on,' Jack said.

Matt looked at him knowingly. 'And you're never far away from it.'

'You mean the Fechter piece? Right place, right time,' Jack said, then thought it wasn't his best turn of expression. 'To be honest, the kid's screams are still haunting me.'

Matt grimaced. 'I can imagine.'

'Not that our boys did much to help.' Jack still felt bitter about the inaction.

'Come on, Jack, what did you expect? You know we can't set foot over there without creating a major incident.'

'It didn't need much. They could have got him out. I was there, remember?'

Matt Collins shook his head then waved to the waiter, gesturing for two more coffees.

'We can't be held responsible for every hothead who decides they want to make a run for the wall... Forgive me if it sounds heartless, but one death, as brutal as it was, sure beats another world war.'

Jack understood the bigger picture. Matt was voicing the prevailing view on the corridors of power in Washington, but not the one from the streets of Berlin.

'Maybe it's better if we talk about something else,' Jack said.

They sat in silence for a moment, watching the waiter snake his way through the occupied tables towards them.

'I don't want to fall out with you, Jack, but we've seen first-hand what happens when things escalate. We've been on the battlefield; hell, some of our friends didn't come back from Korea with us.'

The coffee duly arrived. Matt welcomed it like Jack would welcome a beer at that particular moment. He did wonder why Matt had asked him here when all they seemed to do was disagree about US policy in Berlin. They needed to forget their tiff over a few beers, but Matt always seemed too busy for that these days.

'Nobody wants a war, but our troops have to show they care,' Jack said.

'I didn't see anybody else helping the Berliners after the war. Did you forget about the airlift?'

'It's 1962, Matt. That was nearly fifteen years ago. The world has moved on.'

Matt turned away. Jack wanted to stop the sniping but couldn't help himself. He needed to find a neutral subject on which they couldn't disagree.

'Are you planning to go back to the States any time soon?' Jack asked.

'Not at the moment. It's all hands to the pump right now.'

'That bad?'

Matt nodded.

He looked at his friend, recalling the days they'd sat in that frozen bunker near the Chosin reservoir, waiting for the Chinese to attack. Jack didn't think they'd survive Korea, yet here they were, bickering over coffee in the sunshine. It didn't seem right somehow.

'We should go for a beer,' Jack said, finally offering the olive branch.

Matt smiled, bringing his brilliant white teeth to the fore. 'I'd like that.'

Jack still felt there was something else. There was a reason Matt had invited him here.

'You remember what we talked about last time?' Matt said.

'We talked about a lot of things, disagreeing about most of it, if I recall.'

Matt sighed, looking into the dregs of his coffee. 'A colleague of mine saw Harry O'Donnell the other night.'

Jack was immediately on guard. 'Oh.'

'He'd had a few, Jack.'

He winced inwardly. He'd hoped Harry had been able to rein things in now he had his big break.

'He was doing a lot of talking, to anybody that would listen actually.'

There was already bad blood between Matt and Harry. They'd fallen out over a woman. In fact, the woman Matt had married.

'Well, I know Harry's not exactly your best buddy…'

'It's not about that, Jack.' Matt took off his sunglasses. 'It's about you.'

Jack swallowed. 'Me?'

'Remember what I said about the big news items, how State was watching like a hawk, especially items about the wall…' Matt hesitated and was staring directly at Jack now. 'About escapes and the like.'

The remnants of coffee tasted bitter in Jack's mouth.

'The word is you and Harry are working together on a big project.'

***

Hans looked across the table at Hannah. They were still having frank and open conversations in the apartment. He had feared the place may be bugged, but after giving it the once over, couldn't see any evidence of that.

'You've gone quiet again,' Hans said. 'Why don't we go out for a while and get some air?'

It was stifling hot in the apartment, yet Hannah hadn't seemed to notice.

'I keep coming back to how I've managed to end up in this situation,' Hannah moaned.

He'd been helping Hannah through her predicament, helping her deal with her emotions. After appearing to improve, she had withdrawn into herself again over the last couple of days. With anybody else it might have been possible to predict what was raging in her mind, but with Hannah it hadn't always been that easy. She always seemed to be one or two steps ahead of his thought processes.

'Technically, it's not you, but Miriam. You're just feeling the effects of her choices.'

He'd spoken to the girl in an attempt to help, not that it seemed to have allayed her suspicion of him.

'Yes, and what an effect.' She shook her head. 'I feel like… I feel like I'm being pushed into a corner,' Hannah said, her frustration evident.

'I've done my best, so you don't feel like that,' Hans said, slightly deflated. He had. He'd made sure he hadn't mentioned the idea again since that day in Treptower Park. It didn't need to be mentioned again. It was a decision hanging over all of them. Could they possibly all escape to the West together?

Miriam wasn't aware of the possibility, of course. Hans didn't doubt she would have welcomed it. Perhaps, like Hans at one time, she didn't believe her mother would ever entertain the thought of defecting.

'Yes, but it's there, isn't it? Dangling, teasing.' She sounded spiteful.

'It's difficult to know what to say. We can't deny the possibility exists.'

He was trying to stay neutral. In effect, he was desperate for the green light. All she had to do was say and he would contact Burzin to get things moving. He'd already asked him to plan for that eventuality. Hans couldn't think of a better outcome. Having only recently met this wonderful woman, he wanted to spend the rest of his life with her. If that could be in the West, then that would be something he could only have dared to consider a few weeks ago. Yet she didn't appear ready to agree to go.

Her lips were pursed, her face tense. It was as if whatever Hannah had been brooding over for the last couple of days was about to boil over.

'I resent her.' The words were quiet, yet she sighed, almost glad it was out.

'Miriam?'

She nodded, then put her hand to her mouth. 'You as well.'

'Right,' Hans said, wondering just how to respond.

She looked at him, tears pricking the corners of her eyes. 'Right? Is that all you can say?'

He shrugged. 'I can understand why you feel like that.' In truth he felt hurt.

'Can you? How can you understand when it's so easy for the both of you? You and Miriam want to leave. You've tried once already. Miriam wants to be with that boy. What's in it for me?'

She broke down. He'd never heard her talk like this before. He and Miriam were following their dreams and aspirations, but not Hannah. Everything she had built since the war, everything she had believed in. She believed in the anti-fascist stance of the government; she had good reason to. In spite of that, he couldn't help pointing out some practicalities.

'Have you thought what it will be like for you if Miriam goes and you stay?'

She looked at him as if he were stupid. 'Of course I have.' She softened her expression and reached for his hand. 'I know there will be questions to answer, but to be honest, Hans, I've come through much worse before.'

He was trying to keep a level head, yet in reality, his own emotions were up and down. He knew it was selfish, but he only wanted Hannah to choose the possibility of a new life elsewhere, if only to be with him. He couldn't help feeling she didn't reciprocate the strength of feeling he held for her.

She wiped away the tears and took a deep breath. 'I'll be totally straight with you, Hans, you have shaken me. What I feel for you has knocked me off my stride. I would never have even considered this… *thing* if it hadn't been for you.'

He wanted to speak but no words came out; in any case, she wasn't counting on an interruption. 'Don't get me wrong, family is very important here. There are no Hirschs left. Letting Miriam go would be the hardest thing I ever have to do.'

She took another breath, her eyes on him now. 'Besides that, I want to ask you something.'

She was staring at him intently. Her bloodshot eyes still retained their magnetism and there was no doubt Hans was hooked.

'Would you leave without me?'

CHAPTER 40

AUGUST 1962, WEST BERLIN

It was a traditional *Kneipe* on Rathenower Strasse to which Burzin had directed him. Moabit wasn't exactly his side of town; for Klaus Schultz it was too close to the wall for comfort. He didn't particularly want to be there. Not that he disliked Burzin; he was over that now. It was just that the man, and all that he was associated with, was not somewhere in his past that Klaus preferred to revisit. The thoughts of his lost comrades, and their suffering, were still very vivid in his mind.

The Kapputer Heinrich was quiet. Most of the clientele were old and content to stare into their glass of *Schultheiss*. No sooner had Klaus picked up his own beer did Burzin breeze in, the perennial cigarette hanging from his lips.

The Russian smiled, and even though the smile lacked warmth Klaus knew him well enough to know it was genuine. 'Good to see you, Klaus.'

He simply nodded and they shook hands.

'Let's take a table,' Burzin said. He ordered a beer and two glasses of schnapps.

Settled at the table with their drinks, and out of earshot, Burzin proposed a toast. 'To our remaining comrades.'

Klaus raised his glass and downed the schnapps. He was sure Burzin had made the toast deliberately vague; Klaus was drinking to his own comrades, with no care for whom Burzin had been referring to.

'You're ageing well, Klaus Schultz. The fine West German air suits you well.'

'More than Russia.' They both laughed. 'Building is no stress, only the people.'

'It's a long way from Kolyma, that's for sure,' Burzin joked.

Those days in the gulag as a prisoner of the Russians were desperate times. Burzin had been the camp commandant. In the years since then, Burzin had been rehabilitated in the Soviet corridors of power.

'I was trying to forget,' Klaus said.

'I can understand that. Yet we find ourselves in each other's company once again.'

'It wasn't always in such comfortable surroundings,' Klaus reminded him.

They both drank their beer without taking their eyes from each other.

'So, what brings you to Berlin?'

Klaus had long since learnt it was best to be direct and honest with the man. Whenever he'd turned to him for help, he'd never let him down. Burzin had saved his life in spiriting him away from Kolyma when he did. He'd also freed Ulrich at Klaus's request.

'The man we met on the border last year, your contact.'

Burzin's eyes narrowed slightly. 'What about him?'

'I assume he's still in East Berlin.?'

'I have taken care of him. He's fine.'

'I've spent a lot of time with his comrade, Bernie Schwarzer.' Klaus looked at his hands, feeling awkward. 'I promised Bernie I would do my best to get him out, if he still wants to come, that is.'

Burzin raised his eyebrows. 'Well, that won't be that easy. It's not like it was in the early days last year.'

'You seem to manage to come back and forth at will,' Klaus said.

'Privilege of rank,' Burzin said.

Klaus knew he was in the KGB, or most likely GRU. His motive for helping in the past had been more about the infighting and his enmity for one man.

'I may have a route out for him,' Klaus said quietly.

'Really?' Burzin lit a cigarette with the dying embers of the previous one. 'And you want me to act as a go-between, is that it?'

Klaus felt discomfort. Burzin always had a habit of making him feel indebted. He was right, but Klaus was a proud man and preferred if it wasn't highlighted. In any case, Klaus had also done some of Burzin's dirty work in return.

'I just want to help out some old comrades.'

Burzin shrugged. Smoke filled the space between them as he exhaled. 'Well, it might surprise you to know I wouldn't be averse to putting it to him.'

Klaus felt relieved. There were times when Burzin would have made it as difficult as possible, even placing conditions on the request.

'Tell me how you plan to get him out.'

'A tunnel. I don't know any details.'

'Interesting. You know the security services are becoming efficient at identifying these projects before they come to fruition. How do you know it's not been compromised?'

'I don't.'

'How did you come into contact with the tunnellers?'

Klaus smiled. 'You can't expect me to give you the details.'

'You are asking me to help you, or Erdmann, are you not?'

'Quid pro quo. Some things never change.' Klaus laughed. 'I can't give you any information because I don't know, but I can tell you one thing which may interest you.'

Klaus told him about Gerd, his arrest, and the girl he planned to take out of East Berlin. There was a good reason he trusted him with this information.

'So why tell me all this?' Burzin gestured to the barman for more schnapps.

'Because of the man who interrogated Gerd.'

'Go on.'

'Weber.'

'Not an uncommon name,' Burzin said, unable to hide the fact his interest had been piqued.

'No, but the description fits perfectly.'

The barman was at the table filling the glasses. 'Leave the bottle,' Burzin grunted.

Burzin lifted the glass, dipped it towards Klaus then downed the contents. Klaus did likewise.

'You think he still works for him?' Klaus asked.

Burzin smiled. 'Oh yes, he still works for Dobrovsky.'

***

Jack was worried. The meeting with Matt had left him feeling uneasy. This time it wasn't about their arguments but about Harry O'Donnell. If Matt had found out about the project due to Harry's loose tongue, it wouldn't take long for Pablo and Renzo to get wind of it. That could put the whole operation in jeopardy. Jack had to catch up with him before he did any more damage.

He first returned home to work on a piece he needed to complete. The place was at least empty, so he wouldn't be disturbed. The evening would then be free to track Harry down.

The phone rang, and Jack tutted at the interruption.

'Kaymer.'

'It's Ulrich, Jack.'

He was surprised, usually they would meet, such was his brother-in-law's obsession about secrecy.

'What can I do for you?'

'It's your TV friend.'

Not for the first time that day, Jack had a feeling he wasn't going to like what his brother-in-law had to say.

'Don't tell me, he's been seen drunk in a bar somewhere.'

'Worse than that. He's been shooting his mouth off.'

'I heard the same from a friend earlier.'

'You need to deal with him, Jack. Talk to him.'

Jack feared it could be past that.

'There's another thing.'

'Go on.'

'You said he was short of money, something to do with his divorce.'
'That's what he told me.'
'The word is he's flashing his money around, buying lots of people drinks.' Ulrich paused. 'It's worrying, Jack.'
'Tell me about it,' Jack said.

CHAPTER 41

AUGUST 1962, EAST BERLIN

It was a hot day. Hans had folded up his shirt sleeves as he made his way on foot to Hannah's apartment. He took his time, ensuring he wasn't followed. Anyway, he had much to think about. He couldn't help feeling sorry for Hannah. She'd not asked for any of the cards she'd been dealt. There were occasions in the last few days when he'd felt he was being self-centred, selfish for his insistence on his own escape. Such had been his fanatical wish to get out since the middle of the previous year, the rest of life had passed him by. His focus on his goal had been so intense he'd not seen it looming on his blind side. Then it had hit him. His love for Hannah had appeared when he least expected it, when he was least prepared for it. It had crept up on him whilst his mind had been somewhere else. Then she'd asked him that question.

A few months ago, or even a few weeks ago, he couldn't have envisaged being in this position. Under no circumstances would he have seen his life anywhere but away from the politics of East Berlin. He'd made himself hate the regime and what it stood for. For him, there had been no decision to make. Yet now, he was beginning to wonder if his love for Hannah had enveloped all those negative feelings. Had they really affected his desire to leave? The only answer he could give was an honest one; he didn't know.

He'd been careful to ensure his presence at the Hirsch apartment had not been noted by the Stasi watchers. He didn't want to complicate an already difficult situation and his presence may well have sounded alarm bells somewhere in the security services.

He'd always used the back entrance to the apartment, identifying the watcher, usually at the front, before he did. It was due to this he noticed the change that morning. There was no watcher by the S-Bahn stop, or even by the cigarette kiosk over the road. There was only a van. It was beige-coloured with writing indicating it was from a bakery in the city.

Hans knew the type of van, and it wasn't delivering bread.

***

Miriam had long since finished her breakfast. She'd not eaten much, such was her mounting excitement. She was ticking off the days until her escape. It wouldn't be long now.

Hans Erdmann would be arriving anytime soon; her mother had told her they'd planned to go off for the day. Miriam wanted to get out as well, but certainly not with them. Their closeness made Miriam slightly uncomfortable, and it wasn't only because she still wasn't sure about Hans.

She picked up her bag. 'I'm going now, Mum.'

Her mother met her in the hallway. She held her close. 'Now, don't do anything stupid.'

Miriam rolled her eyes. The same old things fell from her mother's lips.

Miriam knew the call to leave could come at any time. Now the time when she would leave East Berlin had arrived, she was beginning to understand what it might mean. She knew her mother was still coming terms with her decision. From time to time, in the apartment, her mother would grab her and hug her, unwilling to let go. She'd also started to snap at Miriam, something she'd never done before. Miriam was starting to realise things would never be the same again. She was worried she would never see her mother again, but surely that wouldn't be the case; the division of the city couldn't last that long, could it? Strangely, those factors didn't make her doubt the decision she'd made. She was going and that was that.

Miriam had thought long and hard about Hans Erdmann. It had been more than a week since he'd told her about his own escape attempt. She'd checked his story, and whilst it wasn't exactly corroborated by the East German press, not that it ever would be, it had a ring of truth about it. The deception and downright lies from the government were par for the course. He'd warned she'd been followed, which wasn't exactly news to her, but if he had been working for the Stasi, would he have done that? Maybe the story, and the information he'd given her, was part of an elaborate cover to gain her confidence. Now she was thinking too much.

Gerd was never far from her thoughts. She couldn't help wondering what life together would be like in the West. She had packed a few clothes, bare essentials, ready for the time the call came. Her mother had found the bag, which had brought on another tearful showdown. In many ways, Miriam felt detached from the emotion. It was like it didn't matter to her now her decision had been made. The strength she had found in the last few weeks had shocked her. Maybe this was something her mother had seen, too. For the first time, she was beginning to understand how her mother had reacted all those years ago; Jewish and alone on the streets of war-torn Berlin, dodging from one bombed-out house to another, praying for the arrival of the Russians. Miriam's strength of character emanated from somewhere.

'I thought we could all have dinner together tonight,' her mother said, pulling her from her thoughts.

'With Hans?' she blurted out.

'Yes, is that so strange?'

Miriam could think of a number of reasons why it was, but didn't get chance to say; they were interrupted by the door buzzer.

'That must be him now,' Miriam said. She could see the sickly smile on her mother's face. She was happy for her; in spite of all the turmoil, her mother still had a smile; this thing with Hans was softening the blow.

Her mother opened the door.

Miriam wanted to slip straight out but Hans was inside the apartment in an instant, closing the door behind him.

'Hans? What is it?'

His face was taut and serious. He looked at Miriam. 'Get some clothes in a bag. We need to leave.'

She didn't move.

'What is going on, Hans?' her mother pleaded.

'There's no time. There's a van outside. I believe they're here for Miriam. We can't take a chance. We have to go now.'

'Go? Go where?' It was her mother again asking all the questions. 'Who is outside?'

Miriam could only look at Hans. He nodded at her. She could see he was trying to reassure her without scaring her. At the same time, he couldn't hide the urgency in the situation. Miriam knew very well who was outside. She couldn't afford to be arrested, not now.

Her bag was ready. She could go now. Yet it all came down to one thing. Did she trust Hans Erdmann?

CHAPTER 42

AUGUST 1962, WEST/EAST BERLIN

Jack drove over the Ku'damm, dodging the late-afternoon traffic, and found a place to park up. He felt it was the best time to catch Harry O'Donnell, figuring he might be somewhere between work and play. He had to admit he didn't fancy facing Frau Schwarz, Harry's landlady. If she'd been annoyed the last time he'd called on Harry, he didn't want to think how she'd be with Harry having been up to much worse in the interim.

He was fuming with Harry. He'd actually felt sorry for him when he'd complained about the state of his marriage and his lack of a big break. Harry had needed to forget his troubles. Jack could understand all those things to a certain extent. It wasn't so long ago that Jack found it difficult to function without alcohol. Now Jack knew Harry was up to his old tricks, he was mad he was throwing away this opportunity. He'd had two separate warnings in the last twenty-four hours. It meant there wouldn't be many people in West Berlin who didn't know about their project. He had to get to Harry before somebody else did.

As he pressed the buzzer, he couldn't understand what had got into Harry's head. He figured the project would have settled him down, made him focus on something which could earn the money to take some of his worries away.

'You again.' It was a comment, rather than a question. She was dressed in black as if somebody had died.

'Sorry to bother you again, Frau Schwarz, but I'm looking for Harry.'

She scoffed. 'He's gone, Herr Kaymer.' She stepped back to reveal a hallway full of boxes.

'His room's being cleaned. A real job, I can tell you. It will be re-let tomorrow.'

'You've kicked him out?' Jack said warily.

She shook her head. 'God knows I had enough reason to.'

Jack must have looked confused because the dragon felt the need to elaborate. 'He paid up until the end of the month. He didn't even have the courtesy to come himself. He sent somebody around with the money. Young, handsome… still, a bit shifty looking if you ask me.'

Jack wondered if Frau Schwarz saw that in everybody. 'Did he leave another address?'

'He did, as a matter of fact. It's where this lot is heading.' She nodded towards the boxes. 'If I don't leave it on the street first, that is.'

She left to find the address with Jack's mind whirring. What the hell was Harry up to?

She returned, handing him a piece of paper with an air of bewilderment. 'I was so shocked, I took the liberty of checking the place out myself.'

'Shocked?'

'Well, Herr Kaymer, when was the last time you saw the man with any money? He used to scrounge off me to buy his last bottle of whisky. He was always trying to dodge me, rather than pay his rent.'

Jack could think of a number of reasons why anybody would avoid the woman, but his mind was still ticking as he looked at the address.

'Some swanky place on the other side of the Ku'damm. Private concierge, if you please.'

Jack was lost for words. He couldn't imagine Harry could summon up the initiative to move. He only thought he would be searching out his next drink, let alone finding, renting and funding an upmarket place.

'Now, if you don't mind.' She raised her eyebrows then looked down at Jack's foot, which was wedged in the door. It was a force of journalistic habit.

'Sorry.' Jack stepped back. 'Er, when was this?'

'About two weeks ago.' She was looking at him and seemed to take pity on his confused state. 'Look, if you ask me, something stinks, and I don't just mean in his room. How the hell does a drunken layabout like Harry O'Donnell afford a place like that?'

***

It hadn't taken Miriam long to decide. She didn't have time. She'd taken a surreptitious glance down onto the street below to see the van Hans Erdmann had described. If she went out there, they would take her, then Gerd would never be able to get her out, no matter what he had organised.

She ran to her bedroom and took the bag she'd packed. She took one last look around. It was no time for sentiment. She was back in the hallway in an instant. 'Okay, let's go,' she said.

Her mother blocked the doorway, things clearly happening too fast for her. 'Hans, where are you taking her?'

He held her mother by the shoulders. 'It's best not to ask…'

'You can't say that to me, I'm her mother.'

'In an hour, maybe two, when Miriam doesn't appear like normal, they will come up here for her. It's best you know as little as possible, believe me.'

Her mother looked crestfallen. Miriam felt bad for leaving her like this, but she tried to be strong. She kissed her on the cheek. 'I love you, Mum. We'll see each other soon.'

Her mother's expression told her she didn't believe her.

Hans said, 'I'll be in touch when it's safe. They'll question you, so you must be strong. Prepare yourself. I'm sure they don't know about our relationship since the meeting with the students. As for Miriam, stick as close to the truth as possible.'

'Like what?'

'Not that you know she wanted to escape, but about the bad influences she'd been under. The boy from the West. They know it all already, I'm sure.'

He glanced at Miriam and she nodded. The more he said, the more she believed in him.

'I feel alone, Hans,' her mother said. Miriam felt her heart sink.

'Look at me,' he said. 'I have to get your daughter to safety. Once I've done that, I'll be back. I promise.'

'I'm not sure I can lie like that.'

'It's for you, Hannah. For us. If you really want to stay…' He hesitated. Her face brightened for a moment. 'You know what you have to do.'

Miriam gave her mother one last hug, knowing she may not see her again. She closed the door, listening to her mother's sobs, wondering if she'd done the right thing, for the first time.

Hans was waiting outside for her. She looked at him. She was totally in his hands now. In the end, she had no choice but to trust Hans Erdmann.

CHAPTER 43

SEPTEMBER 1962, WEST/EAST BERLIN

There was no jubilation or self-congratulation. In that way, it was very different to the breakthrough on Heidelberger Strasse. It reinforced the professionalism Pablo and Renzo had stamped on the project. They'd reached their target basement – not the original target, of course; that had been changed and kept secret, due to any potential leaks which may have occurred. Now the tunnel was ready.

'For obvious reasons, now we've arrived at this point, none of us can leave this building.' Renzo's serious eyes didn't quite have the same effect on Gerd as when he'd first encountered him, but not far off.

'When do we start bringing people through?' Gerd asked.

'You mean when do you get to inform Miriam?'

Gerd smiled. 'You know it takes time to get a message through.'

'Yes, I do, but as much as I like you, Gerd, we have a deal: everyone on our list comes through first before Miriam is informed.'

Gerd understood. This was the main reason he felt this project would be successful; nothing had seemingly been left to chance. Not that he dared to believe getting Miriam out safely was a foregone conclusion. Too much had happened to think like that.

'The cameramen are in the tunnel doing a full-length walk-through,' Renzo said, somewhat proudly.

Gerd felt a stab of concern, and evidently it showed on his face.

'Don't worry, they won't be allowed to go up on the other side. Pablo is keeping an eye on them. Anyway, O'Donnell is not with them this morning.'

'You really don't like him, do you?'

Renzo shrugged. 'It's not about liking anybody. It's about big mouths messing up months of hard work.'

'What's it like over there?' Gerd was curious.

'We've checked the area out, carefully, of course.'

Gerd was surprised Renzo was risking everything so close to the end, but he had faith they knew what they were doing.

'We have a signalling system in place to inform the couriers when the coast is clear.'

'The area is well guarded?'

'It's always the same. These are restricted areas, as you know. There are constant patrols.'

Gerd was feeling the knots in his stomach now the time was getting closer. 'So it's going to be difficult to get to the tunnel?'

'Ruppiner Strasse and Brunnenstrasse have armed guards in the place where they meet Bernauer Strasse. The apartment blocks on Bernauer Strasse, directly facing the wall, have been evacuated and bricked up, but are heavily guarded. Schönholzer Strasse, one street back from the border, has a roadblock at either end.'

Gerd knew the area – tenement blocks packed in on each other. He sighed deeply. His only thought had been getting the information to Miriam when she had to be ready. All the work he'd completed digging the tunnel, all the efforts of Jack and Ulrich to get him on the team in the first place, felt like more than enough already. Now they were close to the actual escape night: informing people, moving them to the border area, and then escorting them undetected to the tunnel entrance. This was where it could all fall down.

Renzo looked pensive. 'I think we would be naïve to believe the Stasi don't know about the existence of the tunnel.'

'You're really not making me feel any better, Renzo.'

The Italian smiled. 'Do they know about the tunnel?' He shrugged. 'Very likely.' Do they know which cellar we have surfaced in? I believe not.'

Gerd thought quickly, recalling what Renzo had seemingly blurted out some days before. 'It's not Rheinsberger Strasse.'

Renzo smiled cheekily.

Gerd was nodding now. 'And they don't know when you will move the people across?'

It was all making sense to him now. This was all part of the misinformation in case the Stasi did have an informer among their ranks.

Renzo winked. 'You're catching on, Gerd.'

***

Miriam had seen the van waiting for her. It made her feel sick knowing that if Hans Erdmann hadn't have arrived at that particular moment, she would have stepped onto the street completely ignorant to the threat. She could be in a Stasi cell, her dreams of being reunited with Gerd crushed. She glanced at the man on her left. Just who was Hans Erdmann?

Somehow, they'd slipped away from Pankow. They'd stopped at a small kiosk, thankfully shaded by the U-Bahn track above them. Hans returned with a drink which he offered her.

She shook her head, but he insisted. 'It's hot. You need to drink something.'

She'd been oblivious to the sun beating down on them. For the first time since they'd left the apartment, she felt the dampness on her back, the cotton of her blouse stuck to her skin. They had left the apartment via the back courtyard, her arm linked in Hans's as if they were father and daughter. It would have been strange at any other time, but it gave them cover if anybody did see them; the Stasi would only be looking for her alone.

She took the juice and sipped it. 'What will happen to my mum?'

He sighed, seemingly having difficulty hiding his own concerns. 'She's smart, Miriam. I'm sure she'll know what to say.'

She was hit by a wave of guilt. Her mother would be forced to deny she knew anything about Miriam's desire to flee the Republic just to stay out of prison herself. She'd have to distance herself from her daughter and her actions. What had Miriam done?

As if he could read her mind, Hans gave her a nudge. 'It's no time for self-pity. We have to keep moving. He nodded towards the steps leading up to the platform of the U-Bahn on Dimitroffstrasse.

'Is it safe to travel by train?'

He shrugged. 'Act normal, as if we are father and daughter on a day out. There are plenty of people around.'

'What are we going to do, Hans?'

'Like I said, we need to go. I will make a call, organise some things, then…' he looked at her seriously, 'we need to talk.'

Miriam felt uncomfortable, as if under a spotlight. 'Talk?'

Hans's face was stern, leaving her in little doubt. 'I need to know everything. How he contacted you, what this Gerd told you, and more importantly, what's coming next, and when.'

She swallowed hard. Could she tell him everything? She glanced up and down the street, feeling like the place was encroaching around her.

'Let's go,' he said, already heading up the steps to the platform.

***

Jack had been staking out the address Frau Schwarz had given him. The place was on the corner of Pariser Strasse and Sächsische Strasse. There was a café there, the chairs and tables arranged neatly outside and trees lining the seemingly cosmopolitan street. Even though the apartment wasn't geographically far from his last place on Fasanenstrasse, it was clearly a step up. That said, Frau Schwarz had overstated things slightly; for concierge, Jack's would have said caretaker. Using his journalistic nose, he'd already gleaned no apartment in the building was registered in Harry O'Donnell's name.

It wasn't clear what was going on, so Jack had no choice but to sit it out until it was.

Jack was finding Harry's erratic behaviour unsettling. The warnings from Matt and Ulrich were in keeping with the escapades he'd witnessed first-hand; Harry had form for drunken episodes. Yet the largesse around Berlin's expensive nightspots, the sudden change of address, and then property not even registered in his name, or to any recognisable contact of his, definitely wasn't the Harry O'Donnell he knew.

It was still warm, but he didn't want to put the roof down just in case he was spotted. Jack felt his legs becoming stiff after spending most of the evening in the car, so he decided to continue his surveillance on foot. The café's owner had long since stacked away the chairs and tables. It was just after midnight, and if Jack knew Harry, it could well be another few hours before he turned up, if it all.

This part of Berlin was affluent, but also sleepy. There was no one around. Jack was doing his best to stay out of the glare of the streetlights. As he stood in the darkened recess of a shop doorway, a man approached the apartment entrance. Jack stepped back when he saw the man take out a key and enter. He was a young man, good-looking, mid to late twenties. A number of individual apartments used the common door, so the man wasn't necessarily linked to Harry O'Donnell, yet Jack couldn't help sensing he was. It was the first person he'd seen enter or leave the apartment block since an old couple much earlier.

It was only ten minutes later when a taxi pulled up. It was a while before the passenger got out, but when he did there was no doubting it was a slightly worse-for-wear Harry O'Donnell. He seemed to be happy about something, the grin he sported spread across his thin cheeks. Jack thought about intercepting him before went inside but something told him to hold back.

After going through the charade of patting his pockets, Harry gave up searching for his key and pressed on the buzzer. From a distance, perhaps he wasn't as drunk as Jack had seen him previously.

The door opened, briefly bathing the pavement in light. The young man who had arrived ten minutes before was now only loosely sporting a dressing gown. The man stepped back, beckoning Harry in. Seemingly transfixed, Harry stepped inside.

The two men stared at each other, grinning like teenagers. Then, just as the door was closing, Harry reached inside the man's dressing gown and leant forward to kiss him.

CHAPTER 44

SEPTEMBER 1962, EAST/WEST BERLIN

They were off the U-Bahn now. They'd taken two different trains and were walking around a cemetery in Prenzlauer Berg. The warm sun and the unending peace of the graveyard were slightly unnerving to Hans. He'd bought some flowers, which Miriam now carried. It was easy cover; nobody would think twice about grieving relations visiting a gravestone. So far, Miriam had shown a lack of contrition and it was beginning to irk Hans somewhat.

'You didn't have to get involved like that,' the girl said, rather ungratefully.

'No, I didn't.'

'Why then?'

'For your mother. Isn't that obvious?'

The discovery of the Stasi van camped outside the apartment and the spiriting away of Miriam Hirsch to safety were relatively simple tasks. His real worry was for Hannah. He knew what she would face over the next few hours: endless questions about her daughter and how she had been in the run up to her sudden disappearance. Hannah would need all the contacts she obviously had just to retain her liberty. Even if she came through that, she would be a marked woman for a while.

The girl pursed her lips. He could tell she still wasn't sure about him, who he was and why he had suddenly appeared in her life. But this was serious now, and he had to make her understand, for her own sake.

They were silent whilst they passed an old lady chattering intently to a headstone. Hans shivered, thinking about the considerable risk in what they had to do.

He had made the call. Burzin seemed unsurprised by his request for assistance, but for all his grumblings, he agreed to meet them. He found it hard to ask Burzin for anything; he knew there would be a payback – there always was.

'This was never going to be easy, emotionally as well as physically. You understand that now?'

The girl shrugged. Perhaps she was thinking about her mother, but it was no time to be surly and distant. He was growing frustrated and Burzin would not be so accommodating.

Hans stopped suddenly and turned to her, encroaching on her personal space. She seemed shocked, which was exactly what he intended.

'Neither of us wanted it like this. In getting you away, I did what I felt I had to do for your mother.'

She went to interrupt but Hans held up his hand. 'Not yet, you need to listen. You made your choice to leave, and I know that wasn't easy, but you've brought your mother a whole lot of heartache in the process.'

She looked like she was about to cry, but Hans pressed on. 'Your mother doesn't want you to leave, but she sure as hell doesn't want you to end up in Hoheneck either. So, we're here through necessity, not choice.'

She nodded in spite of the tears pricking in the corners of her eyes.

'Now, this boy organising your escape, I have no idea how good the people he is working with are, but whilst they finalise their preparations, we need to keep you hidden. Then we can work out how we will get in contact with them, or if we have to find you another way out.'

Her eyes flashed defiance. 'I will go with Gerd.'

Hans raised an eyebrow. 'At the moment young lady, you are a fugitive and they have no way of contacting you.'

She turned away moodily. Hans was doing his best to keep his anger in check, but the girl was testing his patience.

'Miriam, your only way out of this mess is to trust me.'

She was staring down at the floor as if this was the last place on earth she wanted to be. He could understand her being nervous and uncertain, but there didn't seem to be an ounce of gratitude in her, or even recognition of what he'd just saved her from.

'I feel trapped,' she said, finally. 'It's as if I have no choice.'

In that moment, Hans stopped himself. This was a teenage girl in turmoil. Yet she'd said more than that; her words resonated with him.

After all, he'd felt exactly like that a few months before.

***

Jack had barely slept. More than once during the night, his constant tossing and turning had led Eva to grumble at him. At some stage early in the morning, he'd given up any hope of sleep, got up and tried to piece together what he knew. All the scenarios he came up with were troubling, some more so than others.

It was just before six when he found himself making his way back to Pariser Strasse. It wasn't exactly Jack's time of day. The streets were being cleaned and delivery men were at work, but just as Klaus had reminded him, he wasn't usually out of bed at that time. On the bright side, there was little traffic and it only took him ten minutes to make it across town. Jack was only focused on what Harry was up to, and wasn't going to let it go until he got to the bottom of it.

He only had to wait fifteen minutes before the young man appeared, alone. He was very well dressed, casual yet apparently with style. Jack even wondered if he might be a model of some kind. He was keen to be somewhere. Jack held himself back from taking up the trail. That had to wait; Harry was the priority.

Jack almost choked on the apple pastry he was eating half an hour later, when Harry appeared, looking fresher than he should have done.

He figured he'd been heading for the tunnel and more filming, but that would have to keep for today.

Jack intercepted Harry as he reached out to unlock his car.

'Long time, no speak, Harry.'

Harry looked up in shock. 'Jack, what are you doing here?'

'We need to talk.'

Harry's eyes narrowed. 'Have you been waiting for me?'

Jack sighed. 'It's a bit too late for questions like that.'

'I've no time for riddles, Jack…'

Harry went to get in the car, but Jack forced the door shut.

'Heh! What's the big idea?'

'I figure you'd prefer to talk to me rather than Ricksen, or Jackie?'

Harry look embarrassed for a moment, then nodded rather meekly.

***

The café counter was busy with people heading off to work. Harry had led them there, his demeanour indicating his internal struggles with the conversation he was about to have. They sat, Harry's coffee untouched, Jack slurping at his.

'You tracked me down then?' Harry couldn't keep still.

'The indomitable Frau Schwarz sends her regards.'

Harry had an explanation ready. 'I needed to get away from there. A fresh start.'

Jack only raised his eyebrows.

Harry looked uncomfortable. 'How long have you been watching?'

'Long enough.'

Harry picked up his spoon then put it back down again. 'I… moved in with a friend to save on the rent.'

'You didn't even pay the rent.'

Harry sighed. Jack wondered how long in his life he'd been dodging this question, hiding his real feelings.

'Does Jackie know?'

Harry looked like he was about to deny it, then turned away towards the window. 'She guessed,' he said quietly.

'Who is he?'

He couldn't help the smile that spread across his gaunt features. 'Oliver?'

'The young guy, chin chiselled in stone, no doubt the body, too.'

Harry blushed.

'How long, Harry?'

'With Oliver?'

'I meant men in general.'

Harry looked annoyed now. 'It's not something you switch on and off, Jack. It's always been there.'

'You've kept it well hidden.'

'Well, look at your reaction.'

'My reaction is not about you and men, per se, Harry. It's about the stories I've been hearing. Drinking, telling the world your business.' Jack slammed the table. 'Our business!'

Nobody in the café seemed to notice their confrontation. Jack didn't care anyway, he was just getting going.

***

The People's Park at Friedrichshain was busy. The shrieks of happy children were apparent from a distance. Miriam felt better now that she and Hans had reached some kind of understanding. At first, he'd only seemed concerned about what had happened to her mother; Miriam was, too, but by telling him exactly how she felt, the feeling of being cornered, totally alone, he had softened. Enough so, she had felt comfortable to tell him the full story of what had happened with Gerd. She just hoped she'd read Hans Erdmann correctly.

'Who are we meeting?' she asked.

'An old friend,' he said.

She couldn't help feeling he sounded slightly evasive. 'Will he help me?'

'I'm sure he will.'

Miriam saw Hans focused on a man up ahead. He was casual but smart, in short-sleeved shirt and trousers. He drew leisurely on a cigarette without looking in their direction.

'It's best you leave the talking to me,' Hans said.

Miriam couldn't help raising an eyebrow in his direction.

'We seem to have a little crisis on our hands, Erdmann.'

The man's tone didn't make him sound like an old friend. They walked on towards the Grosser Bunkerberg.

'So, this is the Hirsch woman's daughter?' the man said out of the side of his mouth.

'They were lying in wait for her this morning.'

'Ah, so you're asking me to hide a fugitive?'

'It won't be for long,' Hans said quickly.

'How long?'

'Until they make contact. She's had word it will be in the next few days.'

The man nodded, pulling hard on his cigarette, barely looking in her direction. Miriam felt a stab of concern. The man didn't seem very forthcoming and more reluctant to help than anything.

'And how are they to make contact if she's hidden away?' The tone was sarcastic.

'I'll work that one out.'

'You're forever giving me problems to deal with, Erdmann.'

'You've had the benefit over the years,' Hans snapped back.

Miriam had heard enough. These men were talking about her as if she wasn't there. 'Just a minute!' The two men stopped in shock as Miriam interrupted. 'I thought you said this man was an old friend.'

The man laughed. 'You certainly have your mother's fire, young lady.'

'You know my mother?'

'Oh yes, most people in East Berlin know Hannah Hirsch.'

She wasn't particularly surprised. 'Well, I'm Miriam and I am in need of your help.'

He was quiet for a moment. Hans went to interrupt but the man held up his hand.

'Miriam?' A half-smile crossed his lips as he said the name. 'You already have plans for the escape?'

She nodded.

'Tell me everything,' he said.

***

'So what? I like a drink. So what, I prefer the company of men? What do you want me to say, Jack? I'm still Harry. The same guy that fought by your side in Korea.'

'But are you, Harry?'

'What's that supposed to mean?' There was a flash of anger.

'Who is Oliver, Harry?'

He shrugged, struggling to keep the cheeky grin from his face. 'He does photo shoots.'

'You don't say?'

'Is that jealousy, Jack?'

Jack wanted to grab Harry by the throat. He didn't seem to have any idea about the trouble he'd caused. He let the jibe pass.

'So, he has money?'

'His Dad's a big shot banker. They don't talk, but his mother still takes care of him.'

'Yeah, I've seen the apartment.'

'It's not a crime to have money.'

'I suppose that depends where the money comes from.'

'Now you listen to me…'

'No!' Jack grabbed Harry's hand, squeezing it so he flinched and tried to pull back, without success. 'You listen to me, Harry. You meet this young, handsome man. Why is he interested in you?'

'Oh, come on, Jack.'

'Why? He wants you to move in. You're spending money like it's going out of fashion. You were a broken man, Harry. Once, did you stop to ask yourself why? Just once.'

'Can you let go of my hand?' Harry was indignant. Jack let go and Harry haughtily straightened his sleeve. 'I don't see why I have to answer your questions.' He looked like he was ready to leave.

Jack sighed, wondering how far this had gone. Maybe Harry was right; maybe this was really none of his business. Perhaps he should let the likes of Pablo and Renzo deal with him. Perhaps Harry was in throes of a mid-life crisis and he was nothing worse than an old fool.

'Well, at least you seem happy, Harry.'

His offended face slipped. 'I am, Jack. I am. Work is looking up and Jackie is off my back…'

'Sorry? What do you mean Jackie is off your back?'

Harry hesitated, apparently wondering if he'd said too much.

Sheepishly he said, 'We reached a settlement.'

Jack had a bad feeling, like the worst scenario that had prevented him from sleeping was playing itself out in front of his eyes.

'*You* paid her off?'

Harry wouldn't look at him now.

Jack closed his eyes. 'Oliver paid her off, didn't he?' His head slipped into his hands.

'What did you tell Oliver about the tunnel, Harry?'

***

By the time they'd completed a lap of the park, Burzin had sucked all the information from Miriam. Hans had been worried at first, but as he watched the two of them talking, Miriam precise, Burzin clarifying each point, he felt they had formed a connection. She certainly seemed more comfortable with Burzin than she did with him.

'So, can you help us?' Miriam finally asked again.

Burzin paused to light yet another cigarette. Hans wasn't sure if it was the fifth or sixth since they'd been in the park. His boss inhaled the smoke deeply, then smiled genially.

'Yes, I believe I can.'

Hans felt a surge of relief, but it didn't last long. Burzin turned to him. 'We could have avoided this delay if you'd have briefed me properly in the first place.'

Hans could see Miriam smirking out of the corner of his eye.

'I'm not sure…'

'The boy, Gerd Braun.'

Hans stopped, somewhat confused. 'I only knew the boy's name a few hours ago and wasn't about to mention it on the telephone.'

Burzin had already moved on. 'An irrelevance. Anyway,' the smile returned to his lips, 'There is no problem to contact the people organising Miriam's escape.'

'What?'

'I already know them.'

'You've lost me,' Hans said.

'Less than a week ago, I had a meeting with a man you know in West Berlin.'

Burzin looked at him as if this information should have enlightened him. Hans merely shrugged his continued ignorance.

'Klaus Schultz. The man who helped Schwarzer across the border.'

'Right,' Hans said, still doubtful.

'The boy who was in their escape party that night…'

Hans nodded, vaguely recalling a young man aiding Eva Schultz through the wire.

'Gerd Braun,' Burzin said.

Hans was genuinely surprised. 'So, what did Klaus Schultz want?'

'Ah, well that solves another problem you so blithely dropped in my lap.'

Hans had stopped walking now, Miriam also intrigued by his side.

'He has an escape tunnel for you, and I assume Hannah Hirsch.'

CHAPTER 45

SEPTEMBER 1962, WEST/EAST BERLIN

Harry O'Donnell still believed his relationship with the dashing Oliver was for the long term. It partially restored Jack's faith in his friend; he'd been a middle-aged fool rather than anything more sinister. That didn't stop Jack fearing the worst. He'd immediately contacted Ulrich after hearing Harry's revelations. He just hoped it wasn't too late.

They met in the Tiergarten, not far from the Siegsäule. They walked quickly in spite of the warm sunshine; Ulrich seemed to prefer it that way.

'How bad is it?' Jack asked anxiously.

'Pretty bad,' Ulrich said.

'Oliver?'

'Not easy to follow, which tells its own story. We lost him a few times, but we have watchers posted on each of the checkpoints anyway.'

'He crossed into East Berlin?'

'Not him, but one of the people he met.'

'You think he's Stasi?'

'Without doubt,' Ulrich said. 'It appears O'Donnell has been caught in a classic honeytrap. We've suspected a number of these agents roam the popular clubs of West Berlin listening and watching.'

'And along came Harry…'

'Something like that.'

Jack felt sick. 'So they know about the tunnel.'

Ulrich nodded. 'From what Harry told you, it's likely.'

'Everything?' Jack was incredulous. 'All that work.'

Ulrich grimaced slightly. 'Not everything.'

'What do you mean?'

'We always take precautions.'

'But if they know where the tunnel is?' It seemed hopeless to Jack.

'They don't know where the tunnel surfaces in East Berlin, or when they will start to move the escapees.' Ulrich was deep in thought.

'Do you think we could do anything else to affect it?'

'Maybe. Harry's at your place?'

Jack nodded.

'Do you think he's up to facing Oliver and keeping it together?'

'It's possible. Maybe if you get him angry, help him realise what Oliver has done. A man scorned and all that…'

Ulrich flashed a smile. 'You might make an agent yet, Jack Kaymer.'

Jack scoffed. 'No thanks, I've still got a heart in there somewhere.'

Ulrich laughed. 'That's rich, coming from a journalist.'

The laughter was only momentary, as Jack's mind turned to his friend. 'Where does that leave Gerd?'

Ulrich sighed. 'Ah, yes.'

'What does that mean?'

'It might be better if this came from you.'

Jack's heart sank. 'What came from me, Uli?'

'Miriam has gone missing.'

***

Hans Erdmann had taken her to a disused office at the back of an abattoir. They were in Lichtenberg, close to a large railway junction; the vibration in the office each time a train went by was testament to that. The old office was musty and dank and looked like it hadn't been used since the war. The smell that pervaded Miriam's nostrils made her stomach churn. Hans had stayed with her the whole time, seemingly content with his own thoughts since the meeting with the suave Russian. Miriam's confidence in him had grown slowly, especially now she knew they had the Russian's support. But why would a Russian want to help them escape to the West? It didn't make any sense.

Yet Miriam couldn't help but be excited by what she had heard them discussing earlier that day.

'Do you think she'll come?' Miriam asked.

Hans pursed his lips, seemingly annoyed at the interruption in his thoughts. 'I really don't know, Miriam.'

She sat up quickly. 'Have you planned this all along?'

He scoffed. 'It's far more complicated than that.'

'Like you haven't got time to explain.'

He sighed, then turned away from her, as if he really didn't want to go there, but Miriam wasn't giving up. 'I think you owe me that much at least.' She added a cheeky smile.

He shook his head, then a smile broke the tension. 'Just like your mother.'

'Oh God, I hope not.'

She had him laughing now.

'Where should I start?' He sighed. 'I grew disillusioned with it all along time ago. I was ordered to do things I really didn't agree with.'

'Like what?'

'I'll get to that. I started to pass information to people who I thought could keep the hardliners in check.'

Miriam's eyes opened wide. 'The man we met? But he's Russian.'

Hans nodded. 'I didn't actually meet him until last year, but he was always the one pulling the strings.'

Miriam was amazed so much was going on in her country. She always thought it was so dull. 'So why did you try to escape?'

'The decision to close the border was the final straw for me. The progressives amongst us had clearly lost. There was no point in continuing the fight from inside; it was time to get out.'

'But the man you spoke to is Russian, KGB?'

'GRU, foreign intelligence, but there are many factions and people are always vying for power and influence. Like I said, it's complicated.'

'So, what happened the night you tried to escape? The man said Gerd was there.'

'Burzin, the man you met, organised the escape of my comrade from prison. My payback was to assist Klaus Schultz's daughter, Eva, over the border. Gerd was helping her because she'd been injured somehow.'

It was a strange feeling. Miriam couldn't believe Gerd had been involved in all this stuff from such a young age. She experienced a warm feeling; perhaps it was a sense of pride in what he had done.

'They all managed to escape that night, except me. As you know, I was shot close to the wire…'

'And it was covered up. I saw the newspaper reports.'

'I went back to work as if nothing had happened, except I was made to talk to your mother's students about my work on the border.'

Her eyes widened as she twigged. 'Someone sending a message?'

'Exactly. "We're still watching you."'

'Wow. That's incredible.' She couldn't believe what the man sitting in front of her had been through. He seemed so calm. She felt the excitement she had yearned for before she'd met Gerd.

'I had no idea my mum was planning to come with us. This is amazing.'

Hans held up his hands. 'Miriam, it's not that simple.' His face had turned serious, yet seemingly sad.

The man seemed so complex, like there was still something he wasn't telling her. Then it dawned on her. 'Oh no, she doesn't want to come, does she?'

He sighed. 'You know your mother better than me. This is her home, but far more than that, her heart is here.'

Miriam got up quickly. She slipped to her knees in front of Hans, grabbing his hand. 'But you have to talk to her. We have to talk to her.' She wasn't giving up. 'We have to convince her to come, Hans.'

He nodded slowly, as if he'd been there already. Miriam knew her mother and she could be very stubborn.

'We have to get to her first.'

'What do you mean?'

Worry crossed his face. 'If she hasn't been arrested, they'll be watching her very closely.'

Miriam felt bad, knowing this was because of her. 'But you're trained in that sort of thing. Look how easily you spotted them and got me away.'

For the first time, Miriam could see a tiredness in the man. His greying hair at the temples, which before made him look distinguished, now only intensified an air of fatigue.

She gripped his hand hard. 'We have to try, Hans.'

***

It was a job Jack hadn't volunteered for. Ulrich had organised for him to go to the tunnel. He was met by the Italian, Renzo, close to the Tiergarten, and taken to a factory on Bernauer Strasse. It seemed there was no need for a blindfold now. Renzo knew about Miriam and seemed genuinely sorry for Gerd.

Harry O'Donnell had been fully debriefed. Somehow Ulrich had made him understand the effect of his seemingly innocent pillow talk. Jack knew Harry felt terrible about the trouble he'd caused to the project, and indeed to Gerd and Miriam. He appeared angry enough to put things right and Ulrich was the professional in that particular sphere. In the little he did say about his work, misinformation was one of his few mantras.

Jack was led to his friend, who was resting on a mattress on the upper floor of the factory. He was surprised to see the number of temporary beds lined up. Gerd rested up on his elbow as soon as he saw him. 'Jack, what are you doing…?'

It didn't take a genius to recognise the look on his face.

'What is it, Jack?'

Jack sat down on the mattress. He wondered how many people had worked so hard on digging this tunnel. People were relying on the project to succeed to restart their lives together.

'It's Miriam, Gerd. We've lost contact with her.'

'Arrested?' The word was barely audible, as if he didn't want to consider the awful possibility.

'We don't know for sure. Only the mother is at the apartment, and the surveillance is much more than before.' Jack put his arm around Gerd. 'I'm so sorry.'

Gerd didn't react. His face seemed vacant, the shock still apparent. Renzo turned away. Jack thought he saw tears forming in the Italian's eyes. Maybe he wasn't as tough as he made out.

'How?' Gerd whispered.

'We... don't know for sure.' The last thing Jack wanted to do was tell Gerd about Harry. This wasn't the time. They needed cool heads, not anger. Yet here was the fallout from Harry's lifestyle, from his weakness to alcohol, from his secret life.

'Listen, Gerd, we are doing our best to find her.' The words felt hollow and meaningless. His friend's face was blank. He feared the worst, so he couldn't imagine how Gerd was feeling.

CHAPTER 46

AUGUST 1962, WEST/EAST BERLIN

Klaus Schultz felt genuinely sad when Jack had told him. He had time for Gerd Braun. He was different to the other youngsters, not obsessed with stars and movies, but full of integrity and willing to do anything to help his friends. It reminded Klaus of his comrades. His girlfriend had disappeared, no doubt into the hands of the Stasi. He knew exactly what the boy was going through; he'd experienced it all when they'd taken Ulrich, and then later, Eva. He wanted to do something to help Gerd Braun but felt useless.

In the meantime, Klaus had spent the morning in Viktoria Park with his granddaughter. After an energetic chase between the trees, he'd finally caught her, and with some difficulty, and much against Tanja's will, he'd managed to clip her safely back into her pushchair.

'You look like you've got your hands full, Klaus.'

He didn't need to look up to know it was Burzin. He hated the way he seemed to appear from thin air. Klaus was sure it was a power thing among the espionage community.

'She's a free spirit, just like her mother,' Klaus grumbled.

On looking up, Burzin was puffing away on a cigarette. The smell transported Klaus right back those awful days in Kolyma. He shivered in spite of the temperature.

'It's certainly a wonderful day for a stroll in the park,' Burzin said.

'Only people like you don't stroll in the park for that reason alone.' Klaus immediately regretted his tone. He was always more harsh with the man than he needed to be.

It brought a raised eyebrow from the Russian. 'I've spoken to Erdmann on your behalf.'

'And?'

'It seems a little complicated.'

'How?'

'Straight to the point, Klaus. That's what I always liked about you.'

The birds chirped happily in the trees above them and there was genuine happiness in his granddaughter's face. Burzin's sudden appearance still felt like a cloud over Klaus.

'I believe I have some good news for you,' Burzin said finally.

'He wants to come over?' Klaus had stopped pushing Tanja. Burzin pulled a face, then waited as a middle-aged man panted past them on a bike.

'I'll get to that. No, it's something else… or should I say, someone else.'

It was that moment Burzin chose to take an extraordinarily long drag on his cigarette, another thing that infuriated Klaus about the man.

'The girl, Miriam Hirsch, is safe.'

'That's great news… How did you…?'

Burzin chuckled. 'Let's just say I was helping out an old friend.'

'Wait a minute, how is this linked to Erdmann?'

'Ah, yes, well here's the complicated part. Erdmann has met a woman who he is rather fond of.'

Klaus couldn't make the link. 'Okay. Does he want to get her out as well?'

'Maybe,' Burzin said.

Klaus sighed. Burzin was always two or three steps in front of him, and enjoyed the theatre of a long, drawn-out reveal, and to make people suffer. He wondered how his son could ever have become a spy.

'Miriam is her daughter.'

Klaus felt his mouth drop open slightly. He was having difficulty taking things in. Maybe he should get back to the building game after all. 'So Gerd Braun has been seeing the daughter of the woman Hans Erdmann is… fond of?'

'Exactly.'

Klaus whistled. 'It's a small world.'

'Indeed.'

'So the girl is safe and Erdmann wants to bring out the mother as well? It sounds like a fairy tale,' Klaus said. He saw the grimace on the Russian's face. 'Why do I get the feeling that's not the case?'

'First of all, you need to inform your son the security services are aware of a tunnel in the Bernauer Strasse area. Patrols have been stepped up.'

Klaus shrugged. 'I don't know where the tunnel is, but I will tell him. What else?'

'I have concerns for Erdmann.'

Klaus shot him a look. 'Really?'

'I have a lot of respect for the man, plus he's a valuable asset, and I don't want to drop him in a more difficult situation than he needs to be in.'

Klaus knew this was never going to be straightforward. 'So are you telling me you're going to find another route out for them all?'

'Oh no.' Burzin was shaking his head, almost laughing at the thought. 'I need some token from your side. A gesture which tells me this a genuine enterprise and not some elaborate trap.'

Klaus was getting angry now. 'I'm not part of your game, Burzin. I just want to help a couple of old comrades to get some peace in their later lives.'

'You may not be aware of what other people's intentions are, Klaus. I'm not doubting you.'

Klaus couldn't help pulling a face.

'Look, the tunnel must be close to completion. You will need a courier. They will need to convey information – where to meet the contact to be taken to the tunnel.'

'I thought that's why you were here, so we could arrange all that.'

'I am.'

'Well?'

'I have one condition in all this.'

Klaus rolled his eyes. It had to come. 'The *gesture* you mentioned.'

'Yes, Klaus.' He flicked his cigarette away onto the grass. 'The courier must be someone Hans Erdmann knows.'

***

It was another fine day, which suited Hans. The Lustgarten was suitably busy, and he just hoped it was where Hannah would take her usual mid-morning walk. He realised there would be few opportunities to speak to Hannah. He'd been banking on her contacts and reputation keeping her at liberty. He just hoped she hadn't cracked under the questioning. He knew she was tough deep down and she would need all her strength to stay focused, given the emotional turmoil of the last few weeks. Hans understood Miriam's desire to persuade her mother to come West with them, but he had also realised her mother wasn't a woman who was easily swayed.

He heaved a huge sense of relief when Hannah finally appeared. It didn't take long for her to spot him, or for him to see the obvious tail she'd brought with her, albeit someway behind her. He headed straight to the back of the cathedral and waited for her there. As soon as she came around the corner, out of site of the main Lustgarten, Hans walked towards her. Hannah's face signalled a warning, but he ignored it. Brushing past her, he slipped her a note and immediately left the area. He just hoped Hannah would be able to follow the instructions and lose her surveillance, even for a short time.

Hans quickly made his way down the side of the Altesmusuem and used the wooden bridge to cross the river. Once over the other side, he allowed himself to glance back. Hannah was looking up the river, her demeanour calm. Her surveillance had finally caught up with her but seemed none the wiser to their brief contact.

***

It was two hours later, as planned, when Hannah appeared out of the east entrance of the university, fortunately without her tail. Hans had borrowed a *Kübelwagen* from the barracks pool. It was a risk, but less likely to attract the attention of the Stasi should things get too close for comfort. He waited in a small courtyard at the back of the Altesmusuem, where Hannah was able to slip into the back, lying on the floor by the rear seats. Within minutes, Hans was clear of the area, where he stopped, allowing Hannah to join him in the front.

The two of them embraced, before Hannah pulled away. 'Is she okay? Where is she?'

'She's safe. I'll take you there now.'

Hannah was relieved. 'We don't have long.'

'Long enough,' Hans said. 'We'll get you back before they know you're gone.'

He glanced across at her. She looked tired and drawn, although he imagined he looked a whole lot worse.

'I assume they bought your story,' Hans said.

She nodded. 'I had to call in some favours.' She shook her head. 'It was awful, Hans. The man in charge is an absolute brute called Weber. He was horrible.'

Hans wasn't surprised Weber was involved. He wondered if Dobrovsky might put in an appearance in Berlin.

'But they believed what you told them about Miriam?'

'They were making all sorts of threats about my job, the apartment.'

He knew Hannah had a taster of what many others had suffered, some of which Hans had witnessed first-hand. He couldn't help wondering if it would be enough to make up her mind.

'I can imagine what it was like.'

'They're following me like I'm a criminal.'

'If they thought you were guilty of any crime you wouldn't be here to talk to me.'

She took a deep breath. 'Take me to Miriam, Hans.'

Her face was set. He gunned the engine and headed for Lichtenberg.

CHAPTER 47

SEPTEMBER 1962, WEST/EAST BERLIN

Jack had been forced to leave Gerd with Renzo, as he'd received a message from Ulrich to head back to the apartment. He was worried for his friend. The vacant look of shock hadn't left him yet. He was worried when it did, the anger and despair might lead him to do something stupid, such as heading off down the tunnel into East Berlin. He knew how emotion like that could lead to irrational behaviour; it had affected him when Eva went missing.

Ulrich and Klaus were talking at the table when Jack arrived home.

'We've found Miriam and she's safe,' Ulrich explained.

Jack felt a wave of relief. 'Where?'

Ulrich turned to his father. 'I'll let Dad explain.'

'Burzin has her safe.'

'How is Burzin involved?'

Klaus filled them in on what Burzin had told them about Hans, Miriam and Hannah Hirsch.

'My mother knows the Hirsch woman from the war,' Ulrich said. 'She's quite a woman.'

'We've been lucky,' Jack said.

'Maybe, maybe not. Burzin confirmed they know about *a* tunnel on Bernauer Strasse, but no more detail than that,' Klaus said.

Jack looked at Ulrich. 'Maybe you were right.'

Ulrich shrugged. 'I hope so; in the meantime we have another matter to resolve.'

'There's nothing to resolve,' Klaus said. 'It can only be me.'

Ulrich was shaking his head, so Jack knew there'd already been a disagreement about something, which wasn't difficult with Klaus around.

'Someone care to enlighten me?' Jack asked.

'Burzin has insisted the person who guides them to the tunnel must be someone Erdmann knows,' Ulrich explained.

'Burzin wants me to do it, otherwise he wouldn't have said.' Klaus was adamant. 'He wants me to put myself on the line for Erdmann. He's perverse like that.'

Jack sat back without saying a word. He wondered if Klaus was up to it. There was no doubt he was a tough old dog, but maybe his days of climbing through tunnels was over. He respected Klaus volunteering like that, but he also suspected he wanted to get in on the action; he knew his father-in-law had felt left out.

Ulrich was looking at Jack now. He knew what his brother-in-law was thinking. He knew what Eva would say if she knew.

'Okay, I'll do it,' Jack said.

Klaus looked up, his face more than perturbed. 'Who mentioned you in all this? I mean, does he even know you? You were only stood on the other side of the fence that night.'

'Oh, he knows me,' Jack said.

***

The night had been long and uncomfortable. The lingering smell from the abattoir, and the anxiety she felt, had prevented Miriam from eating any of the food Hans had brought for them. The thought of them all escaping together was paramount in her mind. She hoped Hans could bring her mother here, so she could at least talk to her. Miriam didn't want to believe her mother could pass up the opportunity for them all to be together.

As soon as she heard them, Miriam stood up in expectation. She ran to her, hugging her close. Miriam couldn't hold back the tears. She did wonder how she ever thought she could manage without her.

'Thank goodness you're safe,' her mother said.

'Are you okay? It wasn't too bad?' Miriam managed, wiping away her tears.

'I'm fine. Nothing I couldn't handle.'

Her mother looked around the office, her nose twitching. 'It's to be hoped you don't have to stay here too long,' she said, throwing a look in Hans's direction.

He raised his eyebrows. 'If I recall, your office isn't in much better shape.'

Her mother laughed. It was a relief for Miriam to see her smiling after all the discord of the last few weeks. 'I've missed you.'

'It's only been one night...' Her mother broke off.

Miriam's eyes brightened. 'But you can come with us now?' She looked across at Hans. 'You told her about it?'

Her mother shot Hans a look, this one harsher than the last. He shrugged apologetically.

'It's all so easy for you at your age, Miriam.'

Miriam was beginning to understand the reticence Hans had been showing when she had pushed him about her mother's intentions. Her mother's principles were always sacrosanct.

'Can't you put your beliefs to one side for your daughter?'

Miriam saw the tears in her mother's eyes.

'It's hard for me to explain...'

'But we'll never have another chance like this!' Miriam was pleading now.

Her mother quickly wiped away her tears. 'I've been thinking about nothing else ever since I knew it might be a possibility.'

'So, what's there to think about? It's all arranged.'

Her mother looked towards Hans. Miriam wasn't sure if she was looking for support. To this point, he had said little.

'We leave tomorrow night,' he said.

Her mother sighed. 'It all seems so final.'

'Please, Mum!' The tears were still rolling down her face. The closer she'd come to leaving, the more Miriam was beginning to understand what it would be like to be without her. 'There's no way I can go back home, now. They will arrest me. I have to go! I want you to come with us!'

Her mother cupped her hand under her chin like she always did.

Miriam pulled away in exasperation.

'Look at me.'

She focused on her mother through her tears. 'I promise you I will think hard about this. It can't have come as a surprise to you that I don't share your desire to go West...' Her mother glanced towards Hans. The words were for both of them.

Miriam went to interrupt but her mother stopped her. 'For what it's worth, I believe you should go.'

It made Miriam stop in surprise. Her mother nodded to reinforce what she'd said. 'I will not stop you doing what you think is the right thing. God knows, I wished I'd had the freedom and opportunity to choose at your age. You should go, Miriam, if that's what you really want.'

She sniffled. 'It is.'

She turned to Hans. 'You have to take me back before they know I'm missing.'

'You have to think about this, Mum.'

She held up her hand and turned to Hans again. 'Can you collect me tomorrow night?'

He nodded. 'We can work out a plan to lose the tail on the way back.'

She turned back to Miriam. 'In the meantime, I promise you I will think hard about what you have said. If nothing else, I will get to see you one more time before you go.'

***

Gerd Braun had gone from a broken and desperate state to feeling on top of the world all in the space a few hours. He'd been convinced Weber had taken her into custody, just as he'd threatened, and he'd felt void and empty, as if all his efforts had been in vain. The news that Klaus Schultz had brought back from the Russian was the best he'd ever had. He now knew exactly how Jack had felt the previous year when Eva had been in Stasi custody. He felt emotionally shot, yet when Renzo asked if he'd prefer to leave the tunnel, there was never any prospect of that.

The place resembled a media circus. Cameras rolled in anticipation, awaiting the first escapees at the head of the tunnel. Jack's photographer friend had even ventured into the cellar of the property on Schönholzer Strasse where the tunnel emerged. Renzo and Pablo waited in that property, one at the door, the other at the top of the cellar steps, carrying out similar roles Gerd and Walther had on the ill-fated Heidelberger Strasse tunnel.

Gerd watched as the first woman appeared at the West Berlin end of the tunnel in a fine dress, mud splattered around its hem. Bulbs flashed, almost blinding her, capturing the moment. One after another the escapees emerged from the void of the underground passageway, their arms draped around each other in exhaustion and some celebration. Gerd looked on with mixed emotions. He felt true elation for these people, their meagre possessions dragged behind them. The delight, and relief, after months of planning and fear of failure, or worse still, capture, was etched all over their faces. It brought Gerd a feeling of satisfaction. He had played a small part in this success. He thought about Walther and the others and the pain he'd felt when they'd wrongly accused him, and yet now, it all felt worthwhile.

By the end of the night there were more than fifty people reunited with their families in West Berlin. Champagne corks popped, and glasses clinked in celebration. Yet Gerd felt apart from all that; his mind was focused on Miriam. Jack had volunteered to venture into East Berlin and meet her and Hans Erdmann. He knew that had taken guts from his friend; after all, Jack Kaymer was still a marked man over there. It was a brave gesture, but the same gesture Gerd had made in saving Eva the previous August.

When Renzo appeared, it was nearly three in the morning. The expression of anxiety he wore was not at all what Gerd had expected.

'I thought you'd be pleased. Everything went so well.'

'Like clockwork; I couldn't be happier about that.'

'So what's wrong?' Gerd asked, starting to get worried.

Renzo didn't want to look at him. 'There's a leak in the tunnel,' he said quietly.

CHAPTER 48

SEPTEMBER 1962, WEST/EAST BERLIN

Jack had been up early; he had plenty on his mind. The morning was cooler than the previous days and the damp smell of the approaching autumn hung in the air. He'd been back to Bernauer Strasse that morning. No reports of last night's successful escape had reached the press. Whilst the tunnel remained operational, it would continue that way. This was the night Miriam and Hans Erdmann were to escape, with Jack's help. Yet another hurdle had been placed in their path. The rising water in the tunnel was now ankle deep. The leak had occurred well into East German territory so there was no question of using a pump to at least control the water level, due to the noise it would cause. As if there wasn't enough riding on the escape, it was possible the tunnel may be flooded by the end of the day.

Klaus had sulked for most of the previous evening. He still felt he should be the one to go into East Berlin to assist Erdmann. Yet Ulrich had already planned everything. He had presented Jack with false papers late in the evening, which could only have been prepared as soon as Klaus had informed him of Burzin's demand. Ulrich never had any intention of allowing his father to go. At least Jack had Ulrich's vote of confidence, not that the same could be said for Eva. He'd promised her he wouldn't set foot in the Russian zone again. Although Jack knew, if Eva was to ever forgive him for doing so, it would be because he had been helping Gerd Braun, the boy who had saved her life in Teltowkanal and pulled her through the border fence.

As it was, Jack had few problems passing through Friedrichstrasse station. The surly officer stamped his papers and inserted his daily visa. Jack had no intention of using the papers for the journey back to West Berlin. As he stepped out onto Friedrichstrasse, the propaganda posters welcoming him to the capital of East Germany, the tepid sun was already low in the sky. He felt a chill, wondering what the next few hours would bring.

***

They took a tram to the centre, changing again half way. Miriam was glad to be out in the open air and away from the infernal stench of the abattoir. She was desperate to see Gerd again, but in some ways that had been overtaken by her fretting over her mother's decision. She felt she'd got through to her mother yesterday. Miriam wasn't one for emotional outbursts, and her mother was well aware of that, yet she meant every word she said, and every tear she had shed.

'We'll meet the courier,' Hans whispered, as they sat close together on the tram bench, 'then it's best if I leave you to collect your mother. It's safer if we go separately.'

Miriam didn't really like the sound of being left with a stranger, but it seemed she had no choice. 'Where are we going?'

'I don't know exactly. We'll get our instructions from the person we meet.'

Miriam wasn't comfortable with all the uncertainty, but she understood the reasons. She knew the Stasi picked up information from idle gossip and informants, just like her with Magda.

She now had implicit trust in Hans. He was professional in everything he did. She couldn't even begin to imagine the training required to do the things he did, the smallest of things she would never have thought of, like the flowers in the graveyard. She wondered how his life must have been. Both he and her mother had experienced so much. She knew it affected the way they thought, the way they operated and their decision-making. Yet she still had difficulty understanding why her mother was taking so long to decide about leaving East Berlin.

They alighted in front of the Rotes Rathaus and headed towards the Marienkirche. She noticed the leaves on the trees were on the turn. Hans was apparently too busy checking around them to notice the signs of the changing season. Miriam wondered where else he would have them circling in the next few hours.

They were past the church and heading towards Alexanderplatz when she heard a man's voice next to Hans.

'I'm surprised they sent you,' Hans said.

He was younger than Hans, probably more her mother's age.

'Burzin gave us little choice in the matter,' the man said.

'Either way, it's good to see you again, Herr Kaymer.'

***

Hans raised his eyes to see the train pulling out of Eberswalder Strasse station. He'd picked at the *wurst* he'd bought from Konnopke's snack bar whilst he watched. The plan had been simple enough. Hannah had gone to work at Humboldt University in one set of clothes. Late in the afternoon she would have gone to the toilet, changed, then left by another exit. So far, the surveillance on her had been quite light, but Hans was sure they would have been spooked at losing her the previous afternoon. If it had worked, Hannah would be sitting in the *Kneipe* on the junction of Eberswalder Strasse and Schönhauser Allee. For the last half an hour he'd been watching the bar, Hans had seen no sign of surveillance.

He had no idea if this would be his last day in East Berlin. He was still none the wiser to which way Hannah Hirsch would jump; he'd long since stopped trying to predict her. He shook his head in frustration; this was the perfect opportunity to go, taking the woman he loved with him. He was always wary of thinking too far ahead; it hadn't served him well in the past. Yet he couldn't help visualising how the future might look.

Miriam was reluctant to let him go, but he knew she would be safe with the American journalist. Hans had done a deal with him in the past; he was certain his exclusive story about corruption in the East German government and information about the shoot to kill policy on the border, information provided by Hans, had contributed to the cover-up of Hans's escape attempt. Even though she was a stranger to Kaymer, he was a man of his word.

He crossed the road, lingering long enough in front of the window of the bar for Hannah to see him, even though he couldn't see her, nor did he try. He continued on down the street, turning to see, with immense relief, Hannah leave the *Kneipe*.

'Where's Miriam?' Her face was taut with worry.

'She's with the courier. She's fine.'

'You left her with a stranger?'

He took her hand. 'He isn't a stranger. I know him and she's safe.'

Hannah seemed to calm down. 'Sorry. It's just…'

'I know,' Hans said.

He led her towards Kastanienallee. They had a few hours to kill before they made their way to meet Miriam and Kaymer.

'We should find somewhere to just to get off the streets. Maybe something to eat?' Hans said.

'I'm not hungry.'

'Me neither, but we're better out of the way.'

Everything felt strained between them. He was waiting for her to say something. He couldn't begin to imagine what she was thinking. Maybe she blamed him for being in this position, but he really had no other option. The tunnel was available that night and Kaymer had informed him they had to go earlier in the evening, not early the following morning as they'd originally planned, because there was a problem with the tunnel. He wouldn't mention that to Hannah; she had enough to contend with.

The place on Kastanienallee claimed to be a bistro, yet it was a café at best. Hans ordered coffee, telling the grumpy proprietor they would order food later.

'Is Miriam okay?' Hannah asked.

'She's fine. I'm more worried about you.'

She grimaced. 'This is so hard, Hans. Harder than any time during the war. When my family had gone it was only about me. It was so simple compared to this.'

He took her hand.

'This may be what Miriam wants, but those things are alien to me. Is it my duty to follow my daughter, Hans?'

He didn't answer. He couldn't put himself in her place. He'd only known a few days of being a father. However, he did know he would have done anything to see his son grow up, no matter where that was.

'There is no right answer. If she was a young child, you would make the decision for her.' He paused, not really wanting to say more, yet he knew he had to, if only to maintain the balance. 'She's old enough to take care of herself should you decide to stay.'

Hannah nodded, her lips quivering slightly. 'Then I think about grandchildren and what I would miss.'

Hans smiled. 'I never had you down as the maternalistic type.'

She laughed briefly. Then her head dropped into her hands. 'I could scream right now.'

'Imagine how I feel,' Hans said cheekily.

She gave him that look. 'This is no time for your bad jokes.' Hannah took a deep breath. 'As much as I love Miriam, and as much as I hate myself for saying this, my daughter's decision is separate to mine. It's her choice.'

Hans felt his throat constricting. 'That doesn't make things any clearer to me.'

She shook her head. 'You're going to have to keep up here, Hans Erdmann.'

He shrugged, fearing what was coming.

'As much as it goes against the grain, and I never thought I'd hear myself say such a thing,' she paused, looking into his eyes, 'my decision really depends on what you will do, Hans.'

***

Miriam had worked out the man was American, although his German was nearly perfect, if only with a Berlin accent. He seemed friendly and open, which led her to wonder if all people in America were like that. She felt at ease with him as they waited in a café on Karl-Liebknecht-Strasse for darkness to fall.

'How do you know Hans?' She couldn't help being curious. Miriam knew so little about the man who loved her mother.

'It's a long story. Let's just say he's a good man. I doubt my wife would be with me in West Berlin if it wasn't for him.'

She recalled what Hans had told her about the escape.

'Do you know Gerd?'

The man smiled. 'Yes, he's a very good friend.'

'Oh?'

'He might be young, but he is one of my best friends. He's always there when you need him, and that's why,' he looked around him slightly disdainfully, 'I'm back in East Berlin.'

Miriam laughed. 'You don't like it here either?'

'It doesn't like me, Miriam.'

'Does he talk about me?'

'A lot.'

She couldn't help blushing. The more she heard about Gerd, the more she knew she was making the right choice.

'You don't seem too nervous, if you don't mind me saying.'

'Should I be?'

'You're about to cross an armed border. We'll have to dodge the patrols to reach the tunnel. It won't be easy.'

She shrugged. 'I feel like I'm in good hands.'

He half-smiled then turned away, seemingly with his own thoughts for a moment.

Miriam wondered how Hans was getting on with her mother. She couldn't affect her mother's choice now. She just had to let things unfold.

'Is it far from here?' Miriam asked.

'You ask a lot of questions,' the man joked.

'I like to know where I'm going.'

He nodded. 'I'm sure you do.'

She was still amazed what all these people had said about Gerd. He seemed to have crammed so much into his young life already.

'I'm Jack, by the way,' he said.

'As you're Gerd's best friend, I suppose we'll be seeing a lot of you and your wife in the future.'

CHAPTER 49

SEPTEMBER 1962, WEST/EAST BERLIN

There were no cameras now. In fact, there were very few people around in the factory on Bernauer Strasse. Renzo and Pablo had stayed on with Gerd. They would help him later, when Jack brought Miriam and Hans Erdmann through the tunnel. He was grateful because they didn't have to do that; it wasn't part of their agreement. He just prayed everything had gone to plan and they were all in position.

His biggest worry was the water in the tunnel. He'd been down to the affected area three times during the day. It was eight o'clock now and the water was up to his knees and rising fast. He knew this would be the last night the tunnel would be operational. After that, it didn't matter if it remained undiscovered because it would be completely flooded. That was if it indeed remained passable for the rest of the night.

Gerd had even taken a look in the cellar on Schönholzer Strasse on the other side. It was likely Pablo and Renzo changed the target property mid-project, or at least spread the word it was somewhere different. He had wondered if Ulrich was behind the misinformation campaign. The cellar was still full of suitcases and other items discarded there from last night. Renzo had been amazed by the things people brought, even though they'd been under strict instructions not to bring anything but bare essentials. Gerd shouldn't have been over in East Berlin, but he couldn't help it. He needed to know how everything looked before Miriam and Jack arrived, to check it was still clear.

He glanced at his watch. It was less than two hours until he would finally be with Miriam again.

***

It was dark now. Jack and Miriam made their way from Alexanderplatz through Prenzlauer Berg towards their target. The girl had seemed bright and more relaxed than he had expected. She was sharp and full of questions, but there was no indication of frivolity. Jack had worried she and Gerd were too young to be taking decisions about the rest of their lives, yet now he'd met her, those concerns had waned.

Jack had studied maps of the area over and over. He'd also been well briefed by Renzo and Ulrich. They were now in a small park just off Ruppiner Strasse. They were close to the border and had been warned to expect border patrols. After all, Miriam was a fugitive and there would be an alert out for anyone of her description. If they were stopped, he hoped their story held.

'Okay, we have to act normal. Remember the cover story. We are in a restricted area.'

He handed her the small cake box. She nodded, looking nervous for the first time. 'What about Mum and Hans?'

'He knows where to meet us. We'll make the final run to the property containing the tunnel from there.'

'Will Gerd be at the tunnel?'

Jack smiled. 'Miriam, I imagine wild horses couldn't stop him.'

They left the cover of the trees onto Ruppiner Strasse. There were tenement blocks all around them. To his right, Jack could make out the roadblock at the end of Schönholzer Strasse, and then further on the well-illuminated breezeblock wall which marked the border and Bernauer Strasse. It was quiet. They were the only people on the streets, which made Jack feel exposed. Lights from the apartments lit the ground around them, and the sound of a radio emanated from an open window up ahead.

They crossed the road. Jack peered up at the tall buildings. He recalled the people jumping, risking everything, from windows like these on the border last August. Those apartments facing on to Bernauer Strasse had now been cleared of people, the windows bricked up.

They took a left onto Rheinsberger Strasse and Jack immediately saw two border guards on the opposite side of the road, walking towards them. He felt Miriam tense, but it was too late to turn around now. She linked his arm, daughter and father out visiting. He only hoped it looked like that to the guards.

The guards were only five metres away on the other side of the road. Jack kept walking and praying.

'Halt!' One of the men crossed the road towards them.

Jack heard Miriam let out an involuntary whimper.

***

Hans didn't know how to take Hannah's words. This was a woman who had made the toughest imaginable decisions in order to survive when she was on the run from the Gestapo during the war. Normally, she wouldn't shirk anything. Now she had passed the choice over to him, the dilemma weighing heavily on his shoulders. Leaving East Germany was what he had wanted more than anything. Since the chance had arisen for them all to leave he had dared to believe, but he knew Hannah wasn't at all keen.

He'd been quiet, contemplating everything. Wasn't this an easy decision to make for all of them? Perhaps for him and Miriam it was. He thought about his old friend Bernie Schwarzer. He knew Klaus Schultz had only acted to help because Bernie had pestered him. Bernie would be expecting him to jump at the chance, and he really missed his friend.

Hans sighed. He looked at his watch. 'We should go. They'll be expecting us.'

Hannah grabbed his hand. 'Believe me, I'm ready to do this for Miriam… and for you.'

Hans nodded, but for the first time since he'd known Hannah Hirsch, he didn't believe her.

***

'You know you are close to a restricted area?'

The guard was in his mid-twenties, still moving towards them.

'We've been visiting my sister,' Jack said. He flicked his head, 'on Ruppiner Strasse.'

The guard appeared to be contemplating their story.

Miriam took that moment to edge forward. 'She made us cake.' She nonchalantly held up the box and smiled at the young man.

'It's late to be out,' he said, his eyes narrowing.

Jack shrugged. 'Shifts at work, you know how it is.'

It was then his colleague, who had remained on the other side of the road, flicked away his cigarette and moved quickly towards his comrade. Jack's heart was in his mouth.

The man hissed, but loud enough for Jack to hear. 'For God's sake, Max, can you give it a rest? We're off shift in ten minutes.'

The guard who'd challenged them looked them up and down. It seemed to last an age before he said, 'You should get on home. There are patrols all around here.'

Jack breathed out. 'Of course, comrade. Thank you.'

The guard was still looking at them. Jack pulled Miriam on down the street away from the men.

'Don't look back. Just keep walking,' he whispered.

After a minute Jack allowed himself a casual look over his shoulder. The guards were gone.

'It's clear,' he said.

'How much further?' Miriam asked, the desperation evident in her voice.

He looked over towards the other side of the street, gratefully spotting the archway Renzo had described.

'Over there,' Jack said.

He pulled Miriam over the road and through the arch into a central courtyard. At least they ought to be safe from the patrols here.

Sheets hung on washing lines. Jack tried to peer through them to find the doorway they were looking for. It wasn't easy. A dog barked and a light was switched on, illuminating the yard close to them. He pushed Miriam against the wall, wishing for this all to be over. He looked at the girl. She was petrified. The close shave with the guards had shocked her.

The light went out. Jack felt the sweat rolling down his back for the first time. He was trying desperately to look like he knew what he was doing. The fact was he felt out of his depth.

They found a door, but it was locked. Jack felt desperation for the first time.

Miriam nudged him sharply and pointed to another door. As he pushed down on the handle, he hoped this was the right one.

***

Hans and Hannah left the café after having barely touched the food they'd ordered. They were close to the address on Rheinsberger Strasse Jack had given him. The American had explained they were using a property there only to gain access to Schönholzer Strasse, where the tunnel property was located. Schönholzer Strasse had been blocked at either end due to its proximity to the border, and was constantly patrolled. They had no idea what they were walking into. It was possible the tunnel had been discovered by now; Hans knew there would be other people using the tunnel as an escape route; it only took one of them to make a mistake and the whole operation could be blown.

He looked across to Hannah, who appeared deep in thought. He squeezed her hand. It was time to concentrate on at least getting close to the tunnel. Once there, they could figure out the rest. They turned onto Rheinsberger Strasse. Towards the border, they heard the whining and yapping of fractious guard dogs. Hannah tensed at the sound.

Not far along the street, Hans found the archway he was looking for. On passing through it, they found themselves in a still, silent courtyard, tenement buildings surrounding them.

'Over there,' Hannah whispered.

Kaymer had his head popped out of a door, beckoning them over. At least they'd made it.

It was a relief to be inside. Kaymer directed them down a hallway and one flight of stairs. Miriam was waiting near the doorway, her face pale.

Hannah took Miriam in her arms and held her.

The American looked uneasy, no doubt keen to get the whole thing over. Turning to Hans he said, 'The target property is directly opposite. There is somebody waiting there.'

Hans nodded, barely hearing the words. Now he was here, he wondered what he was going to do.

***

Gerd was standing by the cellar door. Renzo had volunteered to wait at the back of the door leading directly onto the street. Should anything go wrong they would have to flee back to the tunnel. The water was now at waist height on Gerd and nearly up to Renzo's chest. They had one hour, maybe less, before the tunnel would become impassable.

Gerd felt sick. He needed to know Miriam and Jack had made it to the property just over the street. He swore to himself this would be his last escape. He'd taken enough risks in his young life. He just prayed he could get Miriam out.

***

Miriam looked at her mother. She appeared to have aged ten years in the last few weeks and Miriam knew it was all her doing. Now she was here with her, Miriam didn't want to let her go.

'I'm so glad you're here. You are coming, aren't you?'

Her mother could only look towards Hans who was taking final instructions from Jack.

'Mum?'

Jack turned to her before her mother could reply. 'Okay, it's time. Remember what I told you.'

Miriam nodded. 'Why can't we all go across together?'

'It's safer one at a time,' he said, his voice stern. 'You must go first.'

Miriam turned back to her mother, not wanting to let her go. She fell into her chest. 'I love you, Mum.'

'I love you, too, darling.' Her mother lifted her chin and looked into her eyes. 'Now, be strong and do what you have to do.'

Miriam took a deep breath and nodded. Her mother pushed her towards the door.

Jack was looking out onto the street, then he turned. 'Okay, Miriam, it's time!'

***

Jack watched as the girl took a final look behind her, then slipped out into the darkness. The woman had her eyes closed, the tears streaking down her face. Hans Erdmann hugged her. Jack sensed something wasn't quite right.

He peered back out onto the street. Miriam had hesitated in the doorway. He was willing her to get a move on. It wouldn't be long before the next patrol came along. He also had the rising water in the tunnel in his mind now they were here. He'd not mentioned it to her; she was already scared enough.

Then the girl was off in a crouched run making her way to the other side of the road. Jack kept his fingers tightly crossed. He knew Gerd would be in agony waiting for her.

Jack saw the door opposite open briefly and Miriam was inside.

'She made it!' Jack said.

The woman's relief was evident. Erdmann only had eyes for her.

'We need to wait for the next patrol, then I will go,' Jack said. 'You should watch to be sure of the right doorway.'

Erdmann nodded briefly, embracing the woman, not uttering a word. Jack could only imagine what they'd been through over the last few days leading up to this night. For Hans Erdmann, the nightmare had lasted much longer than that. Jack always believed the biggest adventures he'd been involved in could never be written about; nobody would believe him anyway.

He peered out onto the street and saw two guards passing by with a dog by their side. He swallowed hard and thought of Eva and Tanja.

***

Miriam reached the door and an arm immediately pulled her inside. She almost yelped in shock. The man put a finger to his lips.

'Okay?'

She nodded.

He pointed to a door on the left and motioned her on.

At the door, she slipped inside. At the bottom of the steps into a cellar was Gerd. She was down the steps and to him in a flash, throwing her arms around him.

'Thank God, you made it,' he said. 'I thought they'd taken you.'

'If it hadn't been for Hans, they would have done.'

They held each other for a moment. Miriam couldn't believe she'd actually made it here. The whole thing seemed to have gone on forever.

'Are they all there?' Gerd asked.

She nodded. 'With my mother, Hans and the American.'

'We have to hurry. There's water in the tunnel. We don't have long.'
For the first time, she noticed his trousers were dirty and soaked through.
'We have to wait for my mother.'
She looked anxiously towards the door.

**

'I'm ready to go now,' the American said, then he paused. 'Don't forget about the leak in the tunnel. You don't have long.'
Hans nodded his understanding.
Hannah stepped forward and offered her hand. 'Herr Kaymer, I want to thank you for all you've done for Miriam. It was a very brave thing.'
He shook her hand, open-mouthed. 'There's time for all this when we're at the other side, lady.'
'You should go now. We'll be right behind you,' Hans said.
Jack shrugged and was out of the door.
Hans looked at Hannah. She seemed content. No doubt she was pleased her daughter was almost out of danger. He struggled to work her out, her ways, her brilliant mind, but he wanted to keep on struggling. He'd loved every minute of their time together. There was no way he wanted it to end.
He looked out in time to see Kaymer enter the property opposite. He was safely across at least. Hans was grateful for that.
Hannah slipped her hand in his and looked up at him, her head tilted slightly. 'So, Hans Erdmann, what's it to be?'
He looked over the street, wondering if he would ever have another opportunity like this.

EPILOGUE

OCTOBER 1962

They'd made it just in time. At one point, Jack had thought they may have to swim underwater to reach West Berlin. The level had reached his chest, and between them, he and Gerd had pulled Miriam through the deepest water. There was no fanfare on the western side, just a group of exhausted, relieved and bedraggled-looking people. If they had wanted to or not, the decision to retain the tunnel for future escapes had been taken out of Pablo and Renzo's hands. It had served its purpose, for them at least.

In the days afterwards, Jack had pondered if Ulrich's campaign of disinformation had any effect on the Stasi's actions. He'd pushed Pablo to change the target address, even before he knew Harry O'Donnell had passed the information, unwittingly, to the Stasi. Then, on Ulrich's urgings, Harry had told Oliver the escapes had been delayed due to a flood in the tunnel. Again, one of Ulrich's mantras of remaining as close to the truth as possible had played out. More than once during the project, the tunnel had suffered due to flooding, so it was a plausible cover story.

Unsurprisingly, Gerd had taken his time to come around after that evening. Jack knew he'd been badly affected, even burnt by the whole episode. The stress he'd been under during those two months was immense. It was to his great credit he was able to hold it together and bring Miriam through. The girl had impressed Jack with her strength of character. She handled herself brilliantly on the night of the escape, especially when the guard challenged them close to the border. There was no hesitation when it came to wading through the deep water to freedom. Jack had a feeling that whilst there could be some fireworks between Gerd and her in the future, the two of them would be well matched.

Eva remained ignorant of his foray into East Berlin and Jack preferred it to remain that way. The photographs and article had made it into *Newsweek*; Jack was pleased with the coverage, but it wasn't as important to him as it once was. He'd learnt his lesson concerning his career some time ago. Pablo and Renzo were delighted with the additional funds they received by selling Wolfgang's excellent photos to the world's press. It was another daring escape under the Berlin wall, yet the documentary had yet to be aired. At first, Jack wondered if this was due to Harry's ongoing issues, but Matt Collins, now he was finally talking to Jack again, confirmed US government pressure on Harry's bosses had ensured the film remained under wraps, for now at least.

Ulrich Schultz had offered Jack praise for his part in the escape; even Klaus had done so, albeit grudgingly. Klaus was still trying to fathom Hans Erdmann's decision, like all of them who had waited in the cellar at Schönholzer Strasse until it was nearly too late.

***

Hans Erdmann had decided never to look back. He knew the moment Hannah had told him she would follow whatever he decided, there could only be one outcome. A few months before, he could never have imagined he would do such a thing, given all the pain he'd been through to reach that point and indeed, all the effort people had made to put him in that position.

He could not do it. He thought about Bernie Schwarzer but knew he would manage without him. He would get to see his old friend eventually. His decision was for Hannah. He knew she could never live in the West. Her whole life was in East Berlin, among her people, her students, her books.

They'd been very careful to begin with. It took a few weeks, but the Stasi eventually relinquished their surveillance on Hannah. They would always be there, but Hannah could take care of herself and, if absolutely necessary, as a last resort, Burzin was always lurking in the background.

He did wonder if Hannah had planned it; if she knew which way he would jump if she put him in that position. She had the intelligence and wit to do that, but not the cynicism. In the end, Hans didn't care. He believed most of his unhappiness had been about the death of Monika and his son, not about his enemies in East Berlin.

His love for Hannah had overridden it all. Hans knew his life would be good wherever he lived, and Hannah Hirsch was the reason for that.

Additional information

Other books by Paul Grant are also available:

Berlin: Caught in the Mousetrap
https://www.amazon.co.uk/dp/B071G6Q7X7 or
https://www.amazon.com/dp/B071G6Q7X7

Berlin: Reaping the Whirlwind
https://www.amazon.co.uk/gp/product/B077GDBQ8T/ref=series_rw_dp_sw

Berlin: Uprising
https://www.amazon.co.uk/BERLIN-Uprising-Paul-Grant-ebook/dp/B07MTMQS31/

You can find more information about the author online:
www.paulgrant-author.com
https://www.facebook.com/paull.grant.31

Email:
info@paulgrant.com

About the Author

Paul Grant has written three other books, a trilogy about the Schultz family. Below is a link for a podcast Paul recorded with the excellent Cold War Conversations podcast, about the inspiration for his books and future writing plans.

https://coldwarconversations.com/episode46/

Acknowledgements and comments

The world of escapes, and escape tunnels specifically, has always interested me. Throw in the Berlin Wall and it becomes an obsession. The two areas chosen for the book, Bernauer Strasse and Heidelberger Strasse, were the scene of many tunnels and escape attempts, particularly in the first years after the city was divided. This book explores these themes, but also considers the people who chose to stay in the DDR in those early days. In writing this book, I wanted to explore the motivations of people who were more than happy to stay in the DDR and even supported the government's policy to close off the city to those taking advantage of the border situation, or so they perceived it. The book is of course set in 1962. Within the DDR its anti-fascist mantra was one which resonated with many who had been victims of the Nazis. The fact that the West German government had employed former Nazi Party members in some prominent positions further increased support for the DDR's position.

The brave men and women of the escape organisations put themselves at risk of denouncement at every turn. The intelligence network of the MfS of the DDR was one of the reasons tunnelling died out in the later 1960s. A very good source on the subject of the *Fluchthelfer* community is *The Tunnels, the Untold Stories of the Escapes under the Berlin Wall*, by Greg Mitchell. Frederick Taylor's book on the wider story of the Berlin Wall is excellent in understanding the macro picture, as well as drawing on personal accounts of life around this time.

I recommend a visit to Bernauer Strasse and the museum there; they even retain part of the wall and a watchtower over the road from the museum. You can find more information here: https://www.berliner-mauer.mobi/einfuehrung.html?L=1

Printed in Great Britain
by Amazon